"Without question, w[illegible] ce struggles and frustrations that threat[illegible] n ministry. In this relevant book, Charl[illegible] look at these struggles and frustrations based on research and personal experience. Thankfully, he also says we can resist these 'ministry killers,' encouraging us to lead with vulnerability, humility, integrity, and courage. If you are serious about staying focused and faithful in your ministry, read this book and be encouraged."

—Ed Stetzer
President of LifeWay Research

"A delightful guide to anyone in ministry. Just as you need a guide to keep you from making horrific mistakes when you go on a camping trip—mistakes that could embarrass, hurt, or even kill—Charles Stone's book on the *Five Ministry Killers* will make you laugh, cry, and in the end may save your ministry. Get it, read it, enjoy it, and then learn."

—Elmer L. Towns
Co-Founder, Liberty University
Dean, School of Religion
Lynchburg, Virginia

"Charles Stone does a fabulous job of interweaving statistics and stories in *Five Ministry Killers and How to Defeat Them* to make a compelling case for how to defeat those evasive character issues that can destroy a ministry. This is an imperative topic for those of us in ministry today."

—Dave Ferguson
Lead Pastor, Community Christian Church
Spiritual Entrepreneur, NewThing Network

"The book cover promises 'help for frustrated pastors'—and the author has delivered on his promise in a big way. Charles Stone presents relevant statistics, weaves them with stories, and makes it come alive with highly practical advice from a pastor's heart. Reading this book was time well spent."

—Tim Stevens
Author, Pastor, and Blogger
at LeadingSmart.com

CHARLES STONE

5 MINISTRY KILLERS AND HOW TO DEFEAT THEM

Help for Frustrated Pastors—Including New Research From the Barna Group

BETHANY HOUSE PUBLISHERS

Minneapolis, Minnesota

Five Ministry Killers and How to Defeat Them

Cover design by Lookout Design, Inc.

Page 220 is a continuation of the copyright page.

Published by Bethany House Publishers
11400 Hampshire Avenue South
Bloomington, Minnesota 55438

Bethany House Publishers is a division of
Baker Publishing Group, Grand Rapids, Michigan.

Printed in the United States of America

ISBN 978-0-7642-0854-6

The Library of Congress has cataloged the hardcover edition as follows:

Stone, Charles.
Five ministry killers and how to defeat them : help for frustrated pastors—including new research from the Barna Group / Charles Stone.
p. cm.
Summary: "Experienced minister offers insights into frustations pastors face along with solutions, based on current research from the Barna Group and others"—Provided by publishers.
Includes bibliographical references (p.).
ISBN 978-0-7642-0705-1 (pbk. : alk. paper) 1. Pastoral theology. 2. Clergy—Job stress. I. Barna Group. II. Title.
BV4398.S69 2010
253'.2—dc22

2010004285

In keeping with biblical principles of creation stewardship, Baker Publishing Group advocates the responsible use of our natural resources. As a member of the Green Press Initiative, our company uses recycled paper when possible. The text paper of this book is comprised of 30% post-consumer waste.

To pastors everywhere
who labor for their Savior

CHARLES STONE, DMin, serves as senior pastor of Ginger Creek Community Church, in suburban Chicago. He has been in the ministry 30 years, has published numerous articles in church and ministry magazines, and is the coauthor (with his daughter) of *Daughters Gone Wild—Dads Gone Crazy*. Charles has graduate degrees from Southern Baptist Theological Seminary and Trinity Evangelical Divinity School. He and his wife, Sherryl, have three adult children.

To contact Charles for information on his ministry or speaking engagements, visit his Web site: *www.charlesstone.net.*

CONTENTS

INTRODUCTION

Jonathan, who pastored a church in New England for twenty-three years, faced everything from power struggles to salary controversies to questions about his leadership. Once, he confronted some boys in the church after they had taunted several young girls with suggestive comments. His handling of the situation outraged the boys' parents and fueled their resistance toward him.

Another issue swirled around his visitation policy. He knew his greatest primary gifts were preaching and teaching rather than other traditional pastoral ones. So in contrast to what was considered customary, he chose to make a visit only when an emergency arose. However, many members began to fault him for "not loving the people," which further stoked church dissatisfaction.

Fortunately, Pastor Jonathan had a friend, John, upon whom he often leaned. John's stature in that church helped ameliorate many issues that otherwise could have derailed the ministry, and his presence also helped keep criticism at bay. Unfortunately, after John's death, the simmering problems floated to the surface. One particular man was so hostile to Jonathan's leadership that he became the ringleader of a large opposition group.

One final matter became the proverbial straw that broke the camel's back. The previous pastor had loosely allowed unbelievers to become members, and Jonathan later became aware that several of those members had flagrantly sinned. In their small community, these sins had become quite public, and since he believed that only believers who evidenced a changed life should join the church, he began to change the policy.

A firestorm erupted, and Jonathan knew that were he to stand firm on his convictions, he could lose his pastorate. But he stood his ground, and the inevitable occurred. They fired him, and at age forty-six he found himself unemployed. The rejection became so intense that the agricultural town forbad him even to use common grazing land for his farm animals.

One friend, noting how Jonathan responded to his firing, wrote, "I never saw the least symptoms of displeasure in his countenance the whole week, but he appeared like a man of God, whose happiness was out of the reach of his enemies and whose treasure was not only a future but a present good."

Ten years later, because Jonathan had so graciously responded to his critics and his dismissal, one of his main detractors admitted that pride, self-sufficiency, ambition, and vanity had caused the contention. The pastor's handling of his ministry crisis left such an impression that eventually the church publicly repented of their actions, exactly 150 years after they sent him packing.

Who was Jonathan? Jonathan Edwards, arguably America's greatest theologian.[1]

When I first read this story, I was simultaneously shocked and encouraged. Shocked because, as pastor of a midsized church, I too often assume that large-church pastors and influential spiritual leaders don't face the same problems I do. Edwards' story helped dispel my wrong assumption. However, I mostly felt encouraged by his godly response to what could have killed his ministry after he was fired. Because he kept his eye and his heart on what matters most to God, he left an enduring legacy.

That's what this book is all about, encouraging pastors to focus their ministries and their efforts on the issues that matter most to God: loving Him and loving others, and helping those we serve do the same.

When that happens, I believe God will maximize our joy, help us lead at our best, and give us stamina to stay in the game for the long haul. I don't mean to imply that God-honoring strategic plans, state-of-the-art facilities, and well-managed budgets aren't spiritual. They can be and are important. But they don't rise to the top of God's list.

As we'll examine in the pages ahead, minefields that litter ministry threaten to distract us from focusing on what's nearest to God's heart. Although every pastor faces unique challenges, research that I commissioned plainly reveals five significant and common "ministry killers." They are:

1. Head-in-the-sand mentality
2. Misdirected emotional investment
3. Unhealthy responses to ministry killers
4. An attitude that "God and I can handle this"
5. Lonely, hurting spouses

I don't unpack these in a linear fashion (e.g., one chapter per killer). Rather, I've sprinkled them throughout the book and attempted to shed light on them more organically.

Also, my main focus isn't on these factors, in their own right. Rather, particularly in chapters 7 through 10, I emphasize a suggested four-step process that, with God's grace, can help us overcome these insidious killers before they overcome us.

If frustrations are wearing you down, or if you feel you're in the crosshairs, *5 Ministry Killers and How to Defeat Them* could breathe new life into your ministry. It may help you avoid becoming another dropout casualty. It might even bring back some of your joy, if ministry now seems more burden than joy. And if you're new and have not yet faced significant frustrations, you will. Ministry killers lurk in every church, waiting to ambush unsuspecting leaders. This book could help prepare you for what inevitably will come, and help you navigate turbulent waters when they do.

Also, if you're not a pastor or leader, yet what frustrates your pastors and leaders piques your interest, this book might well be for you.

Filled with stories from pastors in the trenches, it's based on groundbreaking, unpublished research gathered for me by three well-known Christian organizations: the Barna Research Group, LifeWay Research, and Christianity Today's NationalChristianPoll.com. The surveys revealed profound insights into what frustrates leaders, how we respond to those frustrations, and what we'd like church people to do differently to help make our service more fulfilling. After sharing the results, I've blended the research into a practical process that can help leaders defeat their *real* enemies.

I pray that God will use these pages to lift the heart of every pastor who faces discouragement. The story that follows lifted mine.

PART I

THIS AIN'T KANSAS ANYMORE

CHAPTER 1

"MAMA ALWAYS SAID LIFE WAS LIKE A BOX OF CHOCOLATES. YOU NEVER KNOW WHAT YOU'RE GONNA GET."

> *I was finally honest with myself: I hated the ministry. I was tired of the lies, the pretending, the guilt, the expectations. I wanted out.* I'm sorry, God, *I prayed.* I gave it my best shot. I tried to do it in your power. It didn't work.[1]
>
> —Pete Scazzero

Pungent almost described the smell. My eyes burned and watered as if I'd walked into a house filled with heavy smoke. The tickle in my throat interrupted my breathing with a dry cough. Every few minutes I squirted antibacterial gel onto my hands; I was reluctant to touch anything. I hoped I wouldn't inhale bacteria beyond my immune system's ability to fight. I turned my eyes from the tumor-filled dog lying in the mud. His labored breathing left a death pall over his body. I felt sick to my stomach.

I fought back tears when a naked little boy, perhaps three years old, ran in front of me, impervious to the shards of glass and rusted cans that littered the ground. This was his playground, his home, his school, perhaps all he ever knew. As I walked between rows of makeshift tin shanties I had to leapfrog streams of raw sewage. I could only look forward to a conversation I would soon have—I needed answers.

This experience occurred in 2008, the year my world got rocked—and not from a family, a church, a financial, or a moral crisis. It wasn't even a personal crisis that caused it—someone I met did. At the time I felt somewhat like the prophet Isaiah when he exclaimed, "I am ruined!"[2]

My life and ministry weren't *ruined* in the common sense of the word. But an encounter with a diminutive black-haired Spanish-speaking single mother who serves Christ in the most despicable place I've ever seen permanently changed me and my perspective on ministry. Challenges that would have killed many ministries in the United States seemed merely to goad this woman to deeper commitment.

In vocational ministry for nearly thirty years, I've tried to encourage pastors through myriad struggles, disappointments, and frustrations. But I couldn't have prepared myself for this one. Hours after the experience above, in Nicaragua, I sat in the Managua Burger King and sipped a Coke. Across the table sat Maria. I felt as though I were in the presence of someone who'd just stepped out of first-century Palestine. I felt encouraged and convicted at the same time as she answered my questions through my translator.

Ten years prior she had watched a TV news report about the many people who actually lived in the city's public garbage dump. She felt God tell her to go and serve them. She hadn't even known where that wretched place (commonly called La Chureca) was located, yet she obeyed. She faced tremendous opposition, not just from the residents there but from other pastors as well. She also gradually discovered she couldn't run her food business in the market and serve full-time simultaneously, so she rented out her market space for $100 per month (just over $3 a day).

I asked Maria about her biggest needs and frustrations. Her replies differed vastly from what mine primarily would have been: books for the other pastors she had trained, food for starving kids, and transportation for herself. She then explained that for years—seven days a week, 365 days a year—she had walked an hour each way from her home, a one-room block structure, to her church in the dump. She had no transportation except her own two feet. Her church now served several hundred families.

That visit stamped a visceral reminder into my soul: *Every pastor faces frustrations, disappointments . . . potential ministry killers.* For most of us, it's not as extreme as the survival of hungry kids or the ability to get to church, but our obstacles are as real and draining to us as Maria's are to her. Her call and passion have burned brighter each year in the face of insurmountable odds. Sadly, many who have heeded God's call with great anticipation to make a kingdom difference have allowed their passion to fade into a flicker. Countless pastors have succumbed to vicious ministry killers, and their dreams lie in graveyards of the soul.

Those dreams can be resurrected and infused with new passion; that's why I wrote this book. Maria shines as one example of how we can experience renewed joy and fulfillment in service despite the bombardments that attempt to kill or cripple us.

I've battled many ministry killers. I've served in churches from the Looney Left Coast (California) to the Windy City (Chicago) to the place where bigger is better (Texas) to the home of the country's best grits and fried okra (Atlanta). The churches have ranged in size from four-and-a-half attendees (the one I started with me, my pregnant wife, and two toddlers) to the one I now serve with over 1,100. Has it been the satisfying experience I expected? Yes and no. To paraphrase Charles Dickens' *A Tale of Two Cities,* "It has been the best of times; it has been the worst of times." Most pastors would agree with Dickens. Many church people would as well.

Living the Christian life and serving God either as a pastor or a church member brings out both the good and the bad—hopefully more good than bad. Unfortunately, current research indicates that many members and pastors are increasingly dissatisfied.

George Barna describes a faction of disillusioned Christians, over twenty million strong, whom he coins *revolutionaries*: "The experience provided through their church, although better than average, still seems flat."[3] He asserts that this growing group is leaving organized churches to find other ways to develop their faith. One Christian magazine noted, "They are not necessarily postmodern twenty-somethings rejecting anything of their parents' generation, nor are they grudge-bearing grumpies carrying an offense from a previous church life."[4]

In early 2007, Ellison Research released the results of a poll on churchgoers' loyalty. Ron Sellers, Ellison's president, found that "in the typical Protestant congregation, one-third of the people in the pews are not definite in their plans to continue attending that church."[5] A 2005 LifeWay study found that "young adults are falling away from church and many are finding church irrelevant to their lives."[6] In 2006, more LifeWay research discovered that the second most common reason people left, behind changes in life situation, was "disenchantment with pastor/church."[7] A recent Pew Research Center study confirmed these shifting patterns.[8]

I *don't* believe the institutional church is going to die. Bill Hybels' oft-quoted mantra, "The church is the hope of the world," resonates deeply with me. I'm convinced pastors can become much more effective and recapture their joy for ministry when they discover their own sub-surface ministry killers, rigorously evaluate them, and begin to act differently in response to them.

By the way, Maria doesn't have to walk two hours each day anymore. Our church met her transportation need and many of her other needs as well. As I become more acquainted with how she joyfully faces barriers and obstructions, I receive fresh hope that any pastor can face his or her frustrations with the same fervor.

Ambitions and Aspirations

Sometimes TV jingles get stuck in my mind. If you're a Boomer and a hot dog lover, you may remember an ad that showed cartoon kids marching and singing in unison about their desire to be an Oscar Mayer wiener, thinking that if they were, everybody would be in love with them. Dog lovers also might recall the Ken-L Ration ditty of the '60s. In this one, a boy's voice extolled the virtues of his dog . . . faster, bigger, smarter, prettier than *your* dog because *his* ate Ken-L Ration.

If we modified these a bit, they might reflect what we pastors sometimes secretly wish. The Oscar Mayer song might go:

Oh, I wish I were a really successful pastor.
That is what I truly want to be.
'Cause if I were a really successful pastor,
everyone would be in love with me.

Or, adapting the Ken-L Ration ditty:

My church is growing faster than your church.
My church is bigger than yours.
My church is better 'cause I'm (emerging, missional, purpose driven, seeker sensitive, expositional . . .).
My church is better than yours.

Of course, most of us would never publicly admit to having such thoughts.

Maybe the obsessive-compulsive Adrian Monk, one of my favorite TV characters, has described life for pastors with his show's jingle, which says life is a jungle filled with confusion and disorder. As much as I believe this may aptly describe ministry, though, Bill Hybels perhaps most accurately captured how pastors feel when at a conference he quoted the platinum song by the Canadian group Prozzäk (of Simon and Milo fame): "Sucks to Be You"!

Have you ever felt that way?

I don't mean to be crass. I don't like that term, never use it, and didn't want my kids to use it. Feels too close to a cuss word. But try as I might to find another expression to describe how ministry can feel . . . *difficult, hard, frustrating, disappointing* . . . *sucks* sums it up best. I bet most honest pastors would concur.

When I say this, I don't mean to be a cynic, nor am I bitter. Again, I've *not* given up on the local church. I'm not having a family-of-origin issue (I don't think) or a midlife crisis (had that ten years ago . . . or was it twenty). But after three decades in vocational ministry and another ten in lay ministry, I've become a realist. Church ministry, and life in general, often disappoints.

I'd really love to believe that everyone in my church is in love with me. But they aren't, and they won't be. All the people in your church are not in love with you either. I'm convinced, however, that even in the midst of trials and disillusionment and potential ministry killers, God can bring us renewed joy. If joy seems elusive in your current situation, once more I pray that God will use this book to rekindle it.

Challenges have checkered my life and ministry. I've been married to my wife for almost thirty years; we've been fruitful and multiplied and have three kids to show for it. One of our children has struggled with the effects of a brain tumor since she was a year old, and she still faces medical struggles. Another gave us five years of grief in her teen years. (Fortunately, she turned around, and we co-wrote a book about it: *Daughters Gone Wild—Dads Gone Crazy*.) Our son attends seminary and sailed through adolescence with few bumps.

I started a church in the South with mega-dreams in my head. I expected to be Atlanta's version of Rick Warren. At our first service, fifty-one people attended. Within six months my successful church plant "grew" to seventeen (twelve if you subtract the five in my family). I believe the offering that day totaled $22.17. A few years later the elders almost fired me, not for a moral failure or malfeasance, but because a critic wanted me out. I've served in an associate role twice, once in the Southwest and once in the far West. In one I had the "Midas touch." In another, I definitely did not.

I never thought I'd even consider the "s-word" to describe church ministry, especially when I think about how I began my career.

God spoke to me.

He really did. I don't mean I heard His voice like I just heard my daughter tell me to look at *Good Morning America*'s report on acupuncture for dogs. But one Saturday morning long ago, He spoke to my heart in a way I've not experienced since.

One weekend, during my last year at Georgia Tech, I'd just returned from a deacons' retreat. I settled into my corner room on the fraternity house's second floor and started an assignment in "Boring Industrial Engineering 401." I had followed my dad's footsteps into engineering, and although it didn't excite me, I did well and planned to attend law school after graduation. I'd taken the entrance test, and with a University of Georgia scholarship offer in hand, I was well on my way to a career in politics . . . until that morning when God spoke.

Words can't fully describe the experience. But I know that at about 10:30 AM, God redirected my life's work into full-time ministry. Afterward I thought, *What could be more exciting? I could study the Bible every day . . . and get paid for it. I could win people to Jesus. I could help them love Jesus more. They would love me. I would love them. And I'd live happily ever after.* How many pastors have started out expecting the same?

I've never questioned God's call that day in my musty Theta Zi room. But some Mondays (and Tuesdays through Sundays), nagging thoughts haunt me: *Am I making a real difference doing this? Does my ministry connect with people's hearts? Do my sermons, on which I spend* twenty weekly hours, *fall on deaf ears?* When I think, *I can't stand church,* do I really mean it? *How long before another person leaves because they aren't "getting fed"? Maybe I* should *have become a lawyer.*

After I've done my best in a sermon, leadership meeting, counseling session, or staff retreat, why do I sometimes struggle with these negative feelings? Why am I frustrated? Why is ministry fulfillment often seemingly elusive?

Am I a carnal, self-centered pastor who's in it for my ego? Do I feel this way because the numbers were down Sunday? Or did those Sonic chili tots I ate Saturday night keep me from sleeping well enough to be refreshed for Sunday's demands?

Was it Jeff (a leader who flipped through his Bible during my entire sermon without giving me eye contact)*? Maybe I didn't get enough "Great message, Pastor" affirmations last week? Was it Sherryl's comment Sunday that I'm better than "all those mega-church pastors"? If I were that good, my church would have ten thousand attendees too.* (She was just being nice. She's my wife.) *Perhaps it was the critical e-mail from William* (one of our key members) *that left me feeling misunderstood.*

So What's the Way Forward?

Sometimes I'm not sure why I feel as I do. If the Barna Group is right about the twenty million who sit in the pews each week, and leave wondering if church is worth their time, then plenty of them probably sit in my church as well.

Low numbers and lack of sleep affect everybody, pastors and parishioners alike. Obviously a major theological dispute, a minister's moral failure or unethical behavior can create dissatisfaction. A church of critics who don't have the church's best interests at heart also can breed it. But the average church probably won't face those issues with the same frequency that we face more common ones—*ministry killers.*

Most pastors are decent people, and I believe most people want the best for their church and their pastors. What, then, causes nagging frustrations? Do they carry latent power that eventually could torpedo our ministries? If so, what can we do about them?

The organizations I commissioned helped me find some answers. Again, the many participating pastors and non-pastors yielded remarkable insights into frustrations that, if left unattended, truly *can* become big problems. The research also discovered how we respond to those issues, and how disconnected pastor and pew often become.

Although these findings give this book objective credibility, please don't expect a stolid research volume or another tome on church growth or conflict management. Don't expect a lecture or "six keys to success." In a down-to-earth way, I want to help open leaders' eyes to reality and to catalyze personal change.

I've learned from both my experience and this research that pastors and church folk often irritate each other. Sometimes pastors don't realize what we do that chafes people. Neither do people in the pew realize what they do that bothers us. Both can be clueless about how the other feels. But when we learn and change how we respond, the joy of ministry truly can increase.

Pastor, I believe you'll find *5 Ministry Killers* will convey hope and challenge. No magical answers. No unrealistic advice. No simplistic solutions. You probably began your ministry as I did, believing you'd make a kingdom difference. That dream may now seem elusive. Perhaps your journey has brought more frustration than happiness, and you wonder if it's time to move on, or out. Search the Web for openings in other churches? Sell insurance? Get your Realtor's license? Try selling burial plots? (One pastor I knew did just that.)

But what if you found a practical plan you could adapt for your situation that could do the following for you?

- Help you discover and articulate your unique ministry frustrations
- Show how to defeat obstacles with the potential to kill your ministry

- Pinpoint the unproductive ways you're reacting to irritations
- Illustrate healthy ways to respond
- Minimize the draining effects ministry places on you and your family
- Demonstrate how to tell your people what they can do to help
- Bring the experience of renewed joy in service to Christ

If those possibilities sound appealing, know that this book will profit you as well as your staff and other ministry leaders. I hope you will find yourself in its stories and come away with fresh fire for your calling.

And for you, faithful church member . . . if you've served for years but now wonder if you should stay . . . if your friends suggest you visit the church down the street and the idea sounds better every Sunday afternoon . . . you picked up *5 Ministry Killers* for a reason. If you understood church from your pastor's perspective and discovered choices you could make to facilitate better leadership, could you enjoy your church more?

Here's the path the book will take. I've organized it into four sections.

Part I presents the case that it behooves pastors to pay attention to what frustrates us before those issues fester and damage us, our families, and/or our ministries.

Part II unpacks the research into three broad areas: what frustrates us most (the killers), how we react, and what we want differently from the people in our churches.

Part III answers the "so what" question: How can we defeat these killers? Here I particularize the research to our own ministries, and each chapter centers on one of four decisions (see diagram) I suggest we must make in response to our frustrations. I believe this process can make us more effective leaders and bring us more joy in our service.

Part IV includes a chapter, dealing specifically with Killer #5, that my wife wrote directly for pastors' spouses. Here I dialogue with Sherryl about her particular challenges.

Note that I often use a masculine pronoun rather than the awkward "he and/or she." Even so, the whole book applies to pastors of either gender.

I've also included two or three reflection questions at the end of each chapter. You might find these useful as you reflect. Or, if you and your staff or board read the book together, these questions might help guide some discussion.

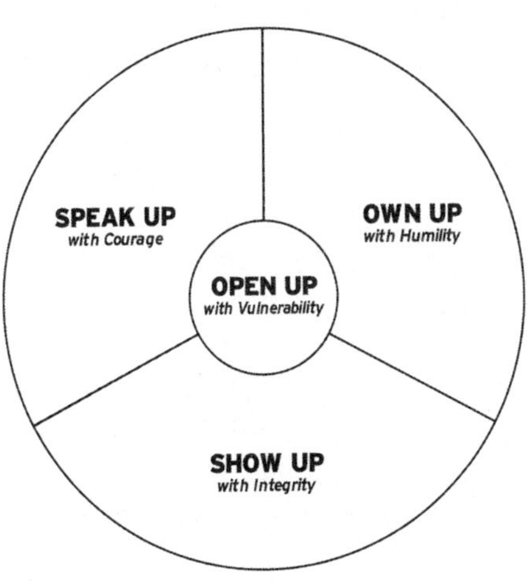

Tom Hanks gave one of his greatest performances in the movie *Forrest Gump*. And almost everyone remembers his now famous words: "Mama always said life was like a box of chocolates. You never know what you're gonna get." Ministry sometimes feels the same. On any given day we aren't sure what our church will throw at us. Uncertainty aside, I don't believe God ever calls a pastor just so dreams and hopes will die. God directs us into ministry to make Him known to others. And in that process, *He wants us to experience His pleasure,* the highest possible satisfaction.

Questions to Ponder

1. What have been the greatest surprises you've experienced in ministry?
2. Have you ever met someone who impacted your life like Maria did mine? What about him or her moved you?

CHAPTER 2

"HOUSTON, WE HAVE A PROBLEM."

The dream of simply walking away, vanishing into the night and when the sun comes up you're somebody new. . . . All your problems are left behind. . . . I looked across the Gulf. There was a lonely little sailboat barely moving on the horizon. And I wanted so desperately to be on it, to sail away to some place where no one knew me. I sat there, watching it move, aching so badly to swim out to it.[1]

—from John Grisham, *The Partner*

A clear Florida day greeted the crew that Saturday in April 1970. Early in the afternoon all systems were *Go* as *Apollo 13* lifted off without a hitch. The anticipation of a third lunar landing was palpable for astronauts James Lovell, John Swigert, and Fred Haise. Aside from a few minor surprises, this looked like the smoothest voyage yet. One crewman on the ground even remarked, "We're bored to tears down here."

Less than fifty-six hours into the flight, the crew finished a forty-nine-minute TV broadcast that showed how they lived and worked in a gravity-free environment. Lovell signed off with the customary "Good night."

Nine minutes later, a most harrowing rescue saga began: the explosion of oxygen tank No. 2 caused tank No. 1 also to fail. Two hundred thousand miles from earth, the command module lost electricity, light, and water supply.

With only minimal battery power, potable water, and oxygen, the crew miraculously returned. The mission eventually would become known as a "successful failure."

The 1995 film *Apollo 13* etched this event into our memory. When Tom Hanks, who played Lovell, grasped their predicament, he spoke these now commonplace words: "Houston, we have a problem" (a slight variation of the actual quote).

What caused this failure? *A tiny part hidden from view set up a chain of events that led to near catastrophe.* Because the service module tanks were so well insulated to contain hydrogen and oxygen, their construction made internal inspection impossible. The contractor had failed to upgrade a simple thermostat that regulated a crucial temperature. As a result, the sensors didn't read correctly, and the tanks exploded.[2] Something minuscule and hidden caused cataclysmic harm to *Apollo 13*.

Pastors in today's ministry culture face problems much like that overlooked thermostat. Events during recent decades have tarnished our reputation. Headlines featuring Jim Bakker, Jimmy Swaggart, Catholic priests, Ted Haggard, and others have skewed the perspective of those we want to reach. In David Kinnaman's seminal book *unChristian*, he isolates six broad themes that reflect how the younger generation now views Christianity. He describes one motif this way:

> *Half agreed that Christianity is hypocritical (47 percent). Mosaics and Busters contend that this is so, not merely because the failures of prominent leaders have been broadcast across their television screens, but also because they are quick to recognize* holes [emphasis mine] *in the lives of people with whom they live and interact.*[3]

When these high-profile leaders stumbled, their "explosions" either killed their ministries or killed their ministry involvement, at least for a time.

The subtle, hidden, overlooked factors that began years prior to erode their hearts seldom received attention, yet they performed their deadly duty.

None of these pastors or priests just decided one day to have a tryst or steal or deceive or simply crash and burn from stress. Slowly, however, tiny and often imperceptible compromises, frustrations, and shortcuts—potential ministry killers—began insidiously to erode their virtues. Little "holes" in any pastor's soul and character, left unaddressed, can bring similar results.

Gary Kinnaman, who served as pastor of a mega-church in Arizona and now consults and writes, aptly describes what sadly happens too often.

> *Everything in the church seems just fine. Everyone seems to be supporting the pastor, and then one day, suddenly it seems, all hell breaks loose. "Where did that come from? How did that happen?" church members ask. "How could such a fine man of God just crash?" But the "sudden" resignation of a wonderful pastor is never, in fact, sudden. It is nearly always the consequence of years of deeply rooted and unrecognized patterns of behavior.*[4]

I lived many years in the South, where banks require a "termite letter" before they'll approve a home mortgage. To get such a letter, the seller must contract an exterminator to examine the home for possible infestation. Sometimes the exterminator can visibly determine damage, if soft wood surrounds windows or siding, or if there are termite trails. But often they must drill small holes into the walls to inspect for unseen damage.

The killers that ultimately cause a pastor to quit ministry, become bitter, or compromise his values are much like termites. Though hidden just beneath the surface, they will eventually bring harm to a leader, his family, and his ministry unless he self-inspects and takes appropriate action. Though tiny in size, killers are deadly in power.

The research that gives the objective foundation for this book provides a glimpse into some of those beneath-the-surface "soul holes." In the book, I don't focus on ministry crises or burnout (though I believe it will edify pastors who currently face them); rather, *5 Ministry Killers* is more about pre-crisis or pre-burnout, with insight akin to what an exterminator would recommend if he were to catch termites early. He might suggest a more detailed evaluation, offer specific treatment, or recommend a handyman to repair damage. I hope I can encourage you to address your frustrations before they lead to personal burnout or ministry collapse.

Once more, these issues don't immediately cause ministries to end, pastors to quit, or marriages to split up. However, keep in mind the termite metaphor. Whether or not the issues seem small now, just like termites, they will cause irreparable damage if left alone, overlooked, or disregarded.

The old anonymous proverb "For Want of a Nail" captures the potential progression following unresolved frustration:

For want of a nail the shoe was lost.
For want of a shoe the horse was lost.
For want of a horse the rider was lost.
For want of a rider the battle was lost.
For want of a battle the kingdom was lost.
And all for the want of a horseshoe nail.

The Research

I've mentioned that the research upon which I've based this book's conclusions has not been previously published. I also reference many other studies on pastoral satisfaction and church life that reinforce the findings. All the same, do keep in mind that statistics can mislead. The year I was born, Darrell Huff published *How to Lie with Statistics*, a quaint but provocative book that cautions us to temper conclusions we may draw from surveys. Sample study, tabulation method, interview technique, question-design bias, question-order bias, sampling error, and respondent deception *can* skew research.

Therefore, *the insights I've drawn will reflect my best understanding of what we can learn and how we can grow to become more effective pastors.* I've tried to let the research speak for itself. Here's a synopsis of the studies; you'll find a more detailed explanation of each in the appendix.

- **Study 1**: In November 2007, the Barna Research Group scientifically surveyed by phone 615 pastors, and asked three questions.
- **Study 2**: In October 2008, the Barna Research Group scientifically surveyed by phone 1,005 U.S. adults (over age eighteen; 650 self-identified themselves as Christian), and asked one question.
- **Study 3**: In October 2008, LifeWay Research (research arm of the Southern Baptist Convention) scientifically surveyed by phone 1,002 Protestant pastors, and asked two questions.
- **Study 4**: In January 2009, Christianity Today surveyed (online) 284 pastors, and asked five questions.

Sprinkled throughout the facts and figures, you'll read honest accounts from real pastors that put human faces on the data. To protect anonymity, I've changed names and altered minor details. Some stories reflect small frustrations. Some reflect big ones. Some have happy endings. Some don't.

Mark's sad tale below, unfortunately, isn't rare. (His story resumes later, however, and brings hope to those who see none.)

Mark's ministry began with great expectations. He spent six years as a student pastor, and then became senior pastor of a seeker church in a growing Midwestern area. As the church began to grow it purchased property and built a building, and many came to Christ. They became so adept at producing a worship service that Mark said, "We could do it even without the presence of God."

Four years into his senior role, a key leader with a stellar reputation crossed a sexual boundary Mark couldn't overlook. He began to apply the Matthew 18 principles for reconciliation, but things didn't go as planned. A friend of the offender, another leader on the board, began to defend his friend, take sides, and create church dissension.

For eighteen months Mark slogged through this experience. He maintained that *love covers a multitude of sins,* but his idealism turned sour. Instead of believers maturing, some became his enemies. Ultimately he found himself "burned out with nothing left to say on Sunday mornings." He resigned and moved to an island in the South Pacific. (I'm not making this up.)

A friend of his, who couldn't fathom what had taken place, asked Mark to try putting into words his experience in a way that would make sense to a non-pastor. It so happened that this friend loved to cook; Mark wrote him a parable.

The Parable of the Cook

Let's pretend that you're a cook, and that you feed the same patrons every week at a buffet. You buy the food, cook it, and the regulars wander in. Some are picky . . . the food is either too hot or too cold. Others complain about items on the menu they don't like. But you love to cook, and your joy for cooking keeps you going.

You begin to notice, however, that many patrons aren't really hungry. Even though they load their plates with food when they arrive, they usually just inspect it and leave most of it untouched. At the end of the line is a donation box to help offset the food cost and, if the patrons are so inclined, to tip you, the cook. Most leave something. Some even give a smile and say thanks. Often it's this appreciation that makes the difference whether or not you keep cooking; being a cook can become very discouraging. . . .

Eventually, the food critics turn their criticism on the cook himself. What once was delicious food has now become bland and boring in their eyes. They even begin to question your motives and character. "Why does he cook, anyway?" some say. Some begin to whine about money. "If he really cares about us, he'll do it without pushing that offensive donation box. He only cares about what goes into the box." They begin to tell other patrons, "We don't need to give the cook money for the food." They even say, "Don't compliment him, because it will go to his head and he won't try to be a better cook."

You slowly begin to go broke. You have to pay your bills, so you get a second job. Eventually, you have little energy left to cook anymore. You still do, but you've lost your joy for it. As the weeks go by people come and load up their plates, but they put little in the donation box and seldom say thanks. They walk away, criticize the food, and talk about how much better the fried chicken is at the diner down the street.

After many months pass, you begin to wonder if these patrons aren't trying to tell you something. You think, Perhaps they want a new cook. *A few quietly encourage you, but for some reason they seem to hide their encouragement from the other patrons. You finally get it. An attitude that can't be changed has overtaken the patrons. They will never be satisfied with you as their cook.*

One day you announce that you're hanging up your apron. The diner will stay open but under new management. As you make your last meal you tell yourself, I'm done with the restaurant business. I'm better off doing something else with my life. *Now maybe you occasionally cook just for your family and for a few genuinely hungry people.*

This illustrates what can happen to pastors overwhelmed by frustration and disappointment. Mark's ministry killers squashed his ability to persevere. But is his story common? Do *many* pastors quit out of frustration or discouragement? Aren't most having the time of their lives?

Do we really have a problem, Houston?

Should *you* be worried, or do these issues usually only affect "the other guys"?

The research I've gathered for this book, plus other data, clearly points to a serious malady, even if at the moment any so-called "killers" seem insignificant. Pastor, you didn't get into ministry to one day get out because you flamed out. We all begin with a sense of call, with substantial dreams, and with a desire to serve the Lord. Ministry entices us partially because it looks so appealing. Blaine Allen framed it well.

> *Ministry. It's nice—is it not?—when it's a suburban, manicured, quiet, well-kept place to come and wash our feet. Nice when there's fruit. When there's encouragement. When there's hope. When there's appreciation. When there's spiritual hunger. When there's readiness to change. When there's passion for Christ. When it's yours, and God blesses and blesses and blesses. It's nice, isn't it?*[5]

We want numerical and spiritual growth, excitement, vision, energy, unity, newness, budgets in the black, and joy. We don't want frustration or disappointment. But the Barna Group survey revealed that a significant percentage of pastors do face frustration that distracts from the main thing. This question, which offered four possible answers, focused on frequency and intensity: *Consider the last year or so and the disappointments or frustrations you may have experienced with the people in your church. Which of the following best describes your experience?*

Response[6]	**Percentage**
My frustrations are frequent and distracting.	8%
My frustrations are frequent but not distracting.	11%
My frustrations are distracting but not that frequent.	38%
My frustrations are neither distracting nor frequent.	38%

These results said nearly half of all pastors deal with ministry frustrations they deem distracting. Ancillary studies report that 67 percent feel emotional stress at least monthly because of the nature of their work,[7] and "only one-third of [pastors] said the amount of fulfillment they get from their job is right where it should be."[8] Focus on the Family estimates from their studies that 80 percent of pastors and 84 percent of their spouses are discouraged or are dealing with depression.[9] Clearly, frustration in ministry is a big deal. Nagging issues drain precious energy from mission-critical tasks.

These drains seem to affect those who pastor smaller churches more than those who pastor larger ones. Forty-eight percent of larger church pastors (*larger* is defined here by attendance over 250) say frustrations are neither distracting nor frequent. Either they assign these issues to other staff, are more mature in how they respond (having learned their lessons earlier in ministry), or are in denial (more about that in chapter 3). This fact is pertinent: Average attendance in the majority of U.S. churches is less than 500 (280,000+ churches). Thirty-four million people attend churches with less than 500; twenty-two million attend churches with more than 500.[10]

Hundreds of verbatim responses revealed how heavily frustrations weigh on pastors. A later chapter categorizes the responses, but this sampling provides a snapshot.

- *Going to church is the people's last priority, if nothing better comes along.*
- *I perceive that most of our attendees want to show up on Sunday and call it good for the rest of the week.*
- *People want a more accommodating God.*
- *I cannot have friends within the congregation.*
- *A consumer mentality fills our church; everything revolves around their kids.*
- *When people make wrong choices and you counsel them, they don't listen to the counsel and they shipwreck their lives.*
- *Some people's attitudes are "What have you done for me lately?"*
- *Strong-willed, control-oriented people assume an ownership attitude of the church and end up creating a disruptive atmosphere.*

And my favorite:

- *People assume the pastor will do everything they need and is available always and is everywhere at all times.*

In addition, other factors compound the problem.

"Pastor, It's Your Fault"

Church attendance in the U.S. is shrinking. Julia Duin, religion editor for the *Washington Times*, writes, "Many evangelical Christians are slipping out or barely hanging on to their churches."[11] Although Gallup polls as late as 2006 showed that church attendance hovers around 43 percent of the population, according to other surveys the figure might be half that amount.[12] Intuitively, when I look around my neighborhood on Sundays, I'd say the lower count matches reality. Duin herself dropped out of church for a while and remarked that when she did, she was "surprised to find out how little [she] missed going to church."[13] Although she has now begun to attend again, her experience reflects how many former attendees feel.

In 2008, the Pew Forum on Religion and Public Life released their Religious Landscape Survey, a 35,000-person poll that examined religion in America. They discovered a large "churn rate," the rate at which people switch churches and/or drop out. Attendance numbers are definitely fading,[14] and the most shocking news, even with moderate growth in conservative churches, is that Protestants have dropped from 60–65 percent of the population in the '70s and '80s to 51.3 percent now. Only 43 percent of those aged 18–29 identify themselves as Protestant.[15]

In 2008, the American Religious Identification Survey interviewed 54,000 people, and *USA Today*, among other news outlets, reported the results. The article captured the study's unsettling result:

> *The percentage of people who call themselves in some way Christian has dropped more than 11% in a generation. The faithful have scattered out of their traditional bases: The Bible Belt is less Baptist. The Rust Belt is less Catholic. And everywhere, more people are exploring spiritual frontiers—or falling off the faith map completely. . . . So many Americans claim no religion at all (15%, up from 8% in 1990), that this category now outranks every other major U.S. religious group except Catholics and Baptists.*[16]

Michael Lindsay, author of *Faith in the Halls of Power*, compiled interviews of 360 Christians at the top of their fields in influence and wrote that they "have lost interest in church because they consider it a waste of their time."[17]

I once heard a well-known twenty-something remark, "I'm so over the local church thing." Many in that age bracket agree with his sentiment, as David Kinnaman (see *unChristian*) discovered. John Eldredge, prominent bestselling author, has given several interviews for *Beliefnet .com* and has been quite candid in his criticism of the local church.[18] He no longer attends one.

Startlingly, disappointment with pastors tops disappointment with other church relationships as a main reason people leave. *Thirty percent* of 1,002 respondents to a 2004 Gallup survey said they'd left a church because they were disappointed with the pastor or minister.[19] LifeWay's 2006 survey discovered that 28 percent of people who'd left for another church left because their church wasn't helping them develop spiritually. As pastors readily know, we usually get blamed for this. (This same study revealed that *43 percent* of those who've left the church left because of an issue with the pastor.[20])

A mostly unintended message telegraphed by recent writings compounds this declining attendance problem by implying that pastors are at fault:

> *Pastor, if you would just teach deeper, lead better, use hair gel, be a more astute cultural architect, become more seeker focused, become more believer focused, be more grace focused, or drink more Starbucks lattes to learn what people are really thinking, then the church wouldn't be in such bad shape.*

Books such as *unChristian, Leaving Church, They Like Jesus but Not the Church, Pagan Christianity, So You Don't Want to Go to Church Anymore, Revolution, A Churchless Faith,* and others do compellingly speak to the state of today's reality. I agree with many of the authors' insights; I even quote some of them. And I don't deny the church's declining influence.

I also believe that the speed of the leader determines the speed of the team, and certainly we pastors own some responsibility for the decline. After all, we can't separate an organization's poor performance from its leadership. But in many ways it seems, now more than ever, pastors are getting blamed for more than they should.

High-Profile Comparisons

If frustration piled onto decline weren't enough, add the tendency for people to compare their pastor with those who lead larger churches. To be fair, we pastors are just as guilty of comparison; adding jealousy to the mix makes for a potent downer. Many small- to medium-sized churches lie in the shadow of mega-churches (those with at least 2,000 in attendance). Scott Thumma and Dave Travis say there were more than 1,250 mega-churches in 2007, and that number is growing.[21] Within a reasonable drive of the church I currently serve are five different mega-churches, one of which plans to locate a multi-site church in our area.

Even without a mega-church nearby, anyone can access outstanding teaching online, through podcasts, or on TV. As a result, many pastors secretly struggle with measuring up to the very successful. One pastor who has grappled with comparison received this e-mail from someone in his church:

> *Hi, Pastor [Jim]:*
>
> *Sharon S. here. How are you? I have been meaning to send you a note for quite some time and tell you about a pastor in California that I thought you might be interested in. Yeah, I know. If I were you I'd be rolling my eyes about now. But I must say, this guy is awesome and has challenged me personally in my life over the last year.*
>
> *He has pastored [God's Favorite] Church just outside [Utopia] for about three years and has grown it from 150 people to over 3,500. I have never seen a young guy with such a passion and a heart for God,*

willing to go against the "appropriate" evangelical grain and just teach the Scriptures.

He just started a new series a week and a half ago. I am going to attach the first message because I would love for you to listen to him. I can't tell you how many people I know listen now. His name is [Gabriel, the archangel]. He has some of the best teaching I have ever heard on leadership in the church, justification, and other tough subjects. He is a lot like [another famous pastor], who is his friend and "fan." Anyway, I have felt led to connect you with [Gabriel] for a long time. I'm not sure why. Take it for whatever it's worth.

Sharon

"Jim" wrote this e-mail response:

Dear Sharon,

Thanks for reminding me that my preaching stinks. It's great to know that people in my church are making sure they get podcasts from somebody who will never know their name or answer their encouraging e-mails.

You've really made my day. I was studying for this week's message when I got your note (I've already spent twenty hours on it). I immediately stopped to download his magnificent sermon. It's also wonderful to know that his church has exploded in growth; as you know, our attendance declined by 3 percent last year because people like you stayed home to watch guys like him on TV!

Gotta go finish my shallow sermon.

God's blessings on you,

Pastor [Jim]

"Jim" didn't really send this e-mail—he only wished he had.

Frustration, church decline, and comparison all contribute to a less-than-fulfilling pastoral experience, and they all can fuel potential ministry killers. And we can't pretend they'll go away. The Hartford

Institute for Religion Research at Hartford Seminary, which studied 4,300 clergy in 1994, found that 32 percent of women and 28 percent of men had thought seriously about leaving church ministry in the preceding year.[22]

One noteworthy quote from the research was given by a pastor who summed up what some people in his church felt about his frustrations: "The pastor should take his frustration and shove it, and pray for his people."

Should we heed such counsel? Those who do, pay a great price. Those who don't will carefully read chapter 3.

Questions to Ponder

1. Would you agree that pastors often get blamed for too many of a church's problems or too much of a church's lack of growth? Why or why not?
2. Have you known any personal friends who, once in the ministry, crashed and burned? What do you think contributed to their fall? Do you see any of those traits prominent in yourself?
3. Is comparison with other successful pastors ever a problem for you? If so, to whom do you compare yourself?

CHAPTER 3

"FRANKLY, MY DEAR, I DON'T GIVE A . . ." (WHY WE'D BETTER GIVE MORE THAN A . . .)

In the United States, numbers impress us. We gauge the success of an event by how many people attend or come forward. We measure churches by how many members they boast. We are wowed by big crowds. Jesus questioned the authenticity of this kind of record keeping.[1]

—Francis Chan

The cliché "Time is money" is quite true for pastors. We're all busy. The week I wrote the first two chapters of this book, I took some vacation days so I could write and do nothing else. Yeah, right. Although I accomplished my goals for that week, church issues interrupted my plans several times. That's ministry life.

One pastor's sentiment from the surveys reflects how many of us feel: "There's too much to do and not enough time to do it." If you agree, you may even be tempted to skim this book to economize time rather than read the whole thing. After all, the average pastor will work fifty-five hours this week.[2] So why should you pay attention and spend precious time on seemingly insignificant frustrations, or even read a book about them? Your plate is already full—why add more work?

Hopefully this chapter will answer that question. I'm convinced that if pastors would identity their frustrations and wants, evaluate them against a healthy standard, and begin to act differently, we could avoid many ministry killers, including burnout.

Many well-known pastors have publicly shared their related experiences. I recently read Wayne Cordeiro's excellent *Leading on Empty*.[3] I've heard Bill Hybels several times refer to his ordeal in the '90s. The book *Mad Church Disease*[4] describes today's pastoral "burnout epidemic."

First Baptist Church of Atlanta was a short walk from my fraternity house at Georgia Tech. In the '70s, I remember Charles Stanley sharing about his burnout struggles. Every pastor who has crossed the burnout line would counsel all of us to avoid it.

Dr. Russ Veenker, who has worked with more than 350 pastors through his Mountain Learning Center in California, which focuses on clergy in crisis, said, "Clergy health *is* the issue at the beginning of the twenty-first century. If we in leadership can model healthy physical, emotional, and spiritual formation—Jesus wins, His church wins, His followers win, and we live abundantly in His joy!"[5]

Remember Mark, the guy who resigned and moved to the South Pacific? His story has a happy ending. After he quit, but just before he moved, a friend invited him to a conference where the speaker challenged pastors, above all else, to develop a deep relationship with Christ. What Mark learned and experienced left an indelible impression.

After his move overseas he began to slowly reenter ministry. Examining his life, he realized that he'd had the "form of ministry, but not its power." As he evaluated his previous performance he began to experience God in a fresh way and his joy began to return. He moved back to the mainland and now feels deeply satisfied in his church work.

As we talked, he said his greatest learning was to keep his focus on God's presence. Before this renewal, ministry frustrations and relational problems would "create an internal offense and debilitate" him. Now he has "yet to find a situation that arises that creates a sleepless night."

Mark paid attention and took action; God renewed his joy and restored him. That's the hope God gives us, whether we're about to bury our ministries, our ministries are about to bury us, or we simply grapple with nagging irritations. Isaiah captured the hope with this promise:

> *To all who mourn in Israel,*
> *he will give beauty for ashes,*
> *joy instead of mourning,*
> *praise instead of despair.*
> *For the Lord has planted them like strong and graceful oaks*
> *for his own glory.*[6]

Daniel Goleman, most known for his work on emotional intelligence, believes every leader can make lasting change for the better. I highly recommend his insightful (co-authored) book *Primal Leadership*. Lasting change "occurs through a discontinuity—a moment of discovery—that provokes not just awareness, but also a sense of urgency."[7]

Mark collapsed under his despair but regained his passion for ministry through an intense experience with God and a healthy journey. But many don't. Although it's difficult to get definitive statistics on pastoral dropouts or terminations, what we do know is sobering. I've summarized some of the findings below.

Who Wants to Become a Statistic?

Forced Pastoral Exits: An Exploratory Study[8] cites several different studies.

- A 1990 study reported that one in four pastors experienced a forced termination.
- A 1984 study of Southern Baptists reported an average of 1,056 involuntary terminations each year. A 1988 study added 400 to that figure.
- A study of 594 pastors in 1996 revealed that 91 percent of them knew of another pastor who was terminated. The study's author confirmed that 23 percent of pastoral respondents had been ousted.
- A 2001 survey discovered that the average tenure of pastors in America is 3.8 years.

Eric Reed, managing editor of *Leadership Journal,* writes that 19,200 pastors annually are required to leave the ministry.[9] A 2003 study[10] for the Religious Research Association gives this statistic: The Evangelical Lutheran Church in America discovered that of 1988's newly ordained pastors, 15 percent had left the ministry in the subsequent thirteen years. The main reasons were feeling stymied, conflict, and isolation.

Christianity Today reported that 22 percent of pastors responding to their 1997 survey have been terminated or forced to leave a pastoral position. Interestingly, *the percentage jumps to 35 percent for those working fewer than fifty hours per week.*[11]

In a study for the Nazarene Church, attrition rates for their ordained ministers totaled 41 percent after fifteen years in the ministry.[12] Focus on the Family estimates that "1,500 pastors leave their assignments each month, due to moral failure, spiritual burnout or contention within their local congregations." They also estimate that 3,000 to 4,000 churches close each year.[13] In 2009, Focus surveyed over 2,000 ministers and discovered that almost 24 percent had faced a forced termination.[14]

Dr. Barney Self, who served several years at LifeWay of the Southern Baptist Convention (SBC), wrote, "I was the repository for information coming from our state leaders who were responsible for forced-termination statistics. The totals were fairly consistent: Roughly 1,200 ministers were terminated each year in the SBC. However, many ministers walk away from the ministry in a very quiet and uneventful way. Consequently, whatever statistics you find will likely be understated. I know ours were in the SBC realm."[15]

Furthermore, this is especially true in regard to younger ministers. In "Provocative Findings on Pastoral Leadership," Dr. Becky McMillan noted, "There appears to be . . . a growing number who drop out of pastoral ministry in the early years of ministry.[16]

The available research indicates that the pastoral survival rate looks abysmal, probably worse than these numbers reflect. But a statistic feels cold until we see a person's face in it. While I was writing this book, a friend who attended seminary with me and later went into ministry reconnected with me through Facebook. Over the years he compiled a list of how his friends who went into ministry fared. Listen to his story:

> *I became a believer in Jesus Christ in 1975. I began attending church immediately, and over the next ten years I went to a denominational college and a seminary in the same denomination. I served on two church staffs and connected with many different ministries, coffeehouses, and churches. I preached in many places and met many people in ministry, many with whom I am still in touch today. If I am not directly in touch, I know what happened to them, where they are, and what they are now doing.*
>
> *When I attended seminary for the first time in the early '80s, John Bisagno, former pastor of First Baptist Houston, spoke in chapel and told us to look around and take a good look at who was sitting next to us. He told an incredible statistic of how few people who start out in ministry will be left after many years. I contacted him to ask exactly what he said. The statistic he told us was told to him in 1953 by his future father-in-law, who was also a pastor. "One out of 10 who enter the ministry at the age of 21 will still be serving at age 65."*
>
> *No way. That seemed staggering, almost impossible to me. I thought of the great need to guard my faith and life, and I never forgot those words and warning. I enjoy staying in contact with people,*

and I began to put together a list of those I met in the first ten years as a believer and the story of their lives since. I continue to add details as I learn them.

The list stands currently at 105 people I knew from my first ten years as a believer in college, ministry, and seminary who were committed to loving and serving God. There are six on my list who were not planning to enter full-time ministry, but they were strongly committed believers in Christ. Those included my first Sunday school teacher, the first person who helped me get into the Word, and the owner of the Christian bookstore where I bought my first Bible. If you had met any one of these people at the time I met them during those first ten years, you would have been inspired and impressed with their commitment to the Lord.

It is now over twenty years later, and it is interesting to see the rest of the story as their lives have unfolded. I am encouraged to know that many are still walking with the Lord and serving Him. I am also grieved and heartbroken over how many have shipwrecked their faith. I believe that the failure statistics are getting worse. What most disturbs me is that these men were all extremely committed to the Lord. This is not the average church or youth group crowd. Thankfully, some of the men who left the ministry, divorced, or failed in other ways are walking with the Lord today and serving Him in some capacity.

I now see how much a person's upbringing and the baggage they bring into their Christian life can impact their adult life, marriage, family, and ministry. Understanding how to deal with this, being set free in Christ, having mentors, and establishing accountability relationships are critical to help people succeed spiritually in their life, family, and ministry.

The following summarizes the results of those in ministry whom I met in my first decade as a believer.

- *In my wedding, there were eight guys, with six of the eight preparing for or already in full-time ministry. Today, four are out of ministry. Five have been divorced, one of them twice, and one who never married has an illegitimate child.*

- *Of the 105 men, fifty-five are still in full-time ministry. Fifty dropped out of full-time ministry, stopped walking with the Lord, or never finished their ministry or seminary training.*
- *A total of twenty-one men are divorced, and four of them have divorced twice.*
- *Among three seminary professors, there are a total of four divorces (the twice-divorced one is currently single again and is also now a seminary professor again; one is the senior pastor of a mainline church, and one is an attorney).*
- *The first Christian bookstore owner I knew (who sold me my first Bible and many other books) is divorced and went bankrupt. He owned the largest Christian bookstore in a large Midwestern city.*
- *My first Sunday school teacher (one of my heroes) divorced his wife after thirty years of marriage and remarried another woman in the church choir.*
- *Three out of four guys at my first Bible study divorced. Two of them are remarried and doing well now in the Lord.*
- *Two are out of ministry because of addiction to prescription drugs and the effects from them.*
- *One was sentenced to ten years in prison. His wife divorced him, and his daughters will have nothing to do with him.*
- *Twenty-two MDiv's and two MRE's are out of the ministry.*
- *Seven who left the ministry had earned a PhD (four) or DMin (three) degree.*
- *Seven of these degreed men are out of ministry for adultery (one included several years of incest). Four of these had an MDiv, and two had a DMin. One had been the newly elected chairman of the Board of Trustees of a denominational seminary, and another the pastor of one of the fastest-growing new church plants in a large denomination in the early '80s.*

When I read how nearly half of these men who began with God's call on their lives to serve Him in ministry are MIA or worse, all the numbers took on different meaning. Again, it's one thing to read a statistic—it's another thing to see a real person behind it.

A Silent Assassin

My house has a basement, and it's recommended that homeowners in our area check their basements for radon. I purchased a detection kit; fortunately it showed normal levels. But to be safe I installed a detector that will sound an alarm if levels rise to the danger zone. Radon is a colorless and odorless gas that will kill you, albeit slowly. It's the second-leading cause of lung cancer, behind only cigarette smoking.

Passion-leak to a pastor is like radon to our lungs. It happens to those who don't cheat on their wives, steal from the offering plate, or shoplift bench saws from Home Depot. It's lethal; it suffocates our souls.

Every day discouraged pastors go through the ministry motions, hoping to find a greener-grass opportunity online. Or they simply get stuck on cruise control until retirement. Drained, defeated, and heart-sick, yet not financially able to quit, their thoughts resemble Elijah's as he ran from Jezebel.

> *When Elijah saw how things were, he ran for dear life to Beersheba, far in the south of Judah. He left his young servant there and then went on into the desert another day's journey. He came to a lone broom bush and collapsed in its shade, wanting in the worst way to be done with it all—to just die: "Enough of this, GOD! Take my life—I'm ready to join my ancestors in the grave!"* [17]

I've been there. Several years ago, during a tough time, I sat on a plane, fortunately at a window seat that afforded me some privacy. I didn't want anyone to see my tears. I wanted to quit the ministry, and on that flight back home I thought about what I could do if I did. Sell real estate? Use my engineering degree to get back into that field? Get a business degree and go into business?

The church I had started hadn't grown much, while other local churches seemed to be thriving. I felt so much like a failure that doing something in which I could succeed seemed to be a way out. Over time, God lifted me out of despair and renewed my passion for ministry. Sadly, though, many pastors don't recover.

Jimmy Dodd leads an organization called PastorServe, which provides counseling and coaching for pastors in crisis;[18] they field 14,000 calls annually. When I interviewed him, Jimmy framed the state in which many pastors find themselves:

> *Many pastors don't think they are called anymore because they have lost their passion for ministry. Most knew it would be hard, and they expected to take some arrows in the chest from the stands. But when they take arrows in the back they say, "That's not what I signed up for. I signed up to stand on the front lines for the kingdom but did not expect to get shot in the back by my own people."*

Every pastor who leaves ministry under dubious conditions doesn't simply decide one day to do whatever "it" was that led him to turn away. Rather, tiny frustrations, broken places, and numbing disappointments insidiously gnawed away until "it" happened and something died inside. Fortunately, most of us have a positive view of ministry that works on our behalf. Christianity Today's NationalChristianPoll.com asked: *When you consider the types of issues that cause the most disappointments or frustrations, would you have entered the ministry?* The response of 300 pastors should encourage us: 65 percent said "Absolutely yes," 29 percent said "Probably yes," and only 5 percent indicated "Probably not."

In a University of Chicago in-person study, 89 percent of pastors said they were very satisfied with their jobs.[19] Compared to other studies this seems high, probably because pastors tend to put on a grin when face-to-face with others. However, Duke University's *Pulpit & Pew* Project has indicated similar satisfaction ratings. In light of other more dismal surveys, one writer astutely asks,

> *How could ministry be seen as such a satisfying vocation, given the reports and stories of burnout and other morale problems, a high drop-out rate in the first five years of ministry, financial struggles among clergy, splits within congregations as well as denominations, and the reluctance of clergy to encourage others to consider ordained ministry as a vocation? The news [seems] Pollyannaish, if not deceptive.*[20]

So how do we reconcile the apparent conflict? And why is this seemingly high satisfaction rating important? The same author provides a credible answer:

> *Might it be that clergy find ordained ministry to be a satisfying vocation in principle, in spite of the enormous obstacles, challenges, and systemic distortions which make it so difficult in practice? After all, my wife and I know from our own involvement in congregational ministry how deeply satisfying and rewarding it is to be invited to share in the lives of other people. Ordained ministers are invited into some of the most intimate times of people's lives—the joys of marriage and new babies and anniversaries and promotions and new jobs, the grief of broken relationships and deaths and the loss of work and tragic systemic injustices.*[21]

I believe this high satisfaction we ascribe to ourselves does provide a strong foundation to help us persevere when times get tough. We've sensed God's call to serve Him and others. This sense gives us an idealistic, *in principle,* satisfaction even though we'd often rate our practical, "in the moment," satisfaction much lower. Our hope and drive to reach the ideal can become a powerful motivator for us to prevail.

Ministry Will Become More Difficult

As ministry becomes harder and more complicated in our culture, the likelihood increases that more pastors will join the ranks of the 46 percent who said frustration distracts them from mission-critical tasks. Here's what I believe the future holds.

Doing Less With Less Will Become the New Paradigm

Bad economic news recently has headlined every newscast and newspaper. More than half of pastors surveyed by LifeWay said the economy was negatively affecting their church.[22] In one large suburban area a pastor friend told me most churches saw an average 20 percent income decrease. I knew of at least three mega-churches that, within a short span, had to significantly cut staff because giving decreased. My church also had to cut staff.

Many have been forced into doing ministry with fewer full-time, paid pastors. That either means workloads will increase for current staff or churches will have to do less and focus on doing a few things well. Apparently some mega-churches already understand this; they have "the lowest ratio of pastors and staff to attendees."[23]

Even preceding the present economic crisis, church donations as a percentage of personal income have been declining for some time. The recent book *Passing the Plate: Why American Christians Don't Give Away More Money*[24] documents the trends. And, one of our most respected business gurus believes our lean times may become permanent.

When CNN recently interviewed Jim Collins, who authored *Good to Great* and *Built to Last*, the content focused on the changing economic climate. In reference to the great companies he'd studied and their challenges, Collins commented on the new reality:

> *It turns out that 1952 to 2000 was an aberration. We had a combination of tremendous stability brought on by two monolithic superpowers—danger, yes, but stability, combined with unprecedented prosperity. Very rarely in human history—maybe the Egyptian empire or*

AD 200 in Rome—can you go back and find those. So my own view is that the possibility of seeing this again in our lifetime is very, very low. What we're experiencing now—get used to it! It's life, and it's the normal life.[25]

Churches will be forced to adapt to decreasing revenues or at least revenues that increase more slowly than before.

The Shrinking Job Market Will Bring Added Stress

The new economic reality will directly affect opportunities for pastors to find jobs. Thirty-five percent of seminary grads find it difficult to get a suitable ministry job within two years of graduation.[26] Even by economizing in other budget areas, churches will shrink hiring plans to reflect tightening finances. More pastors may be forced into part-time positions, thus requiring them to work other jobs. Many may have to take less-than-ideal positions as the labor market narrows. Of course, some will begin new churches, which brings a whole new level of stress and frustration (as well as opportunity).

Patricia Chang, Assistant Director of the Boisi Center for Religion and American Public Life at Boston College, believes many seminary grads will not find jobs in medium to larger churches like the ones in which they grew up.[27] Chang also discovered that most pastors will spend most of their working lives as assistant or associate pastors with limited opportunity to advance to senior positions.[28]

Technology's growing influence will bring leaders unprecedented challenge to keep the shortened attention spans of their people. The remote control has become a pastor's greatest enemy, as Alan Nelson highlights:

As people become more mobile, prefer video to print, and get their info in sound bites and mouse clicks, conventional means of preaching and

> *Bible study are becoming less effective. The "Googling" of America means that people are drawing more and more of their spiritual content from Internet sources, regardless of the quality. The typical church service may be the last place in America where so few have the attention of so many. The ability to preach for 20 to 40 minutes each week to a somewhat static, captive audience flies in the face of what's happening in our culture, where people move to a new Web site when the download requires more than a few seconds.*[29]

Add doses of postmodernism, the emerging/emergent movement, gay marriage, pluralism, time demands, increased mobility, land-use prohibitions against church buildings, biblical illiteracy, increase in fractured families, global warming, and Bigfoot sightings, and pastors *will* face unprecedented challenges and frustrations. The compounding of these issues reinforces our need to pay attention to small yet insidious irritations and respond to them in healthy ways.

What's at Stake?

Joy overwhelmed me as I nestled newborn Tiffany in my arms for the first time. Our third-born was our "surprise" child. Sherryl had experienced her easiest pregnancy, and we enjoyed a problem-free first year, until that fateful second Christmas.

We would often spend Christmas in the small town of Laurel, Mississippi, with my wife's parents. I would joke with my friends that the best vacations for me consisted of all-you-can-eat buffets, long naps, and big-screen TV football. Our Mississippi trips gave me exactly that experience, until that year.

Christmas Day arrived with the expected commotion three excited preschoolers bring. Sherryl's dad strategically placed the old beta video camera to capture their expressions as they dashed into the living room to see the gifts Santa had brought. After we thanked Jesus for Christmas, we watched as they ripped into the colorfully wrapped packages. After they opened the last gift we finally moved to the kitchen for breakfast.

The two older kids sat at the table while I took high-chair duty with thirteen-month-old Tiffany. As I tricked her into eating pureed sweet potatoes and scrambled eggs, I noticed something unusual: her right eyeball quivered, reminding me of someone with Parkinson's. It concerned us, so we saw a pediatrician the next day. The doctor told us not to worry but suggested we see a pediatric eye specialist. When we returned to Atlanta, he gave her a CT scan and said he'd call if he saw anything unusual.

We tried not to worry on the drive home from the doctor, but the ringing phone jarred us as we walked through the front door. I picked it up to hear the doctor's voice; he tried to break the news as softly as he could, but not much could cushion his words. I felt like someone had kicked me in the groin when he said, "Your daughter has a brain tumor." Now over twenty years later, Tiffany has survived four brain surgeries, multiple therapies, and even experimental treatment. She is doing moderately well, though she still struggles.

That Christmas morning I could have ignored her quivering eye. I could have kept it to myself. I could have convinced myself it was no big deal. At that time, the problem did not outwardly affect her in any way, so why bother? But if I hadn't paid attention and then acted, the deeply imbedded tumor would have grown into her brain stem and possibly taken her life or at least permanently debilitated her.

Issues that get under a pastor's skin work in a similar way. They begin as small irritants and frustrations, but if ignored they will continue on a trajectory that could slay a ministry. Much lies at stake if we think these matters are of no consequence. The pastoral fallout rates speak for themselves.

Tiffany's tumor began as a single cell sometime before birth. Similarly, our frustrations, although initially tiny, can alert us to potential ministry killers. Should they morph from irritants to corrosives, they can erode our relationships with our families, with fellow leaders, with church people, and with God himself.

What might be some clues that your trajectory points toward danger? Obvious signs of burnout or depression may include major health problems, paranoia, feelings of hopelessness, extreme exhaustion, yielding to pornography, or marriage struggles. But *pre*-burnout clues are much more subtle.

Read the questions below and answer honestly. If you answer yes to some, please dig deeper and take action. Consider some of my suggestions in parts II and III.

- Does free-floating anger lie just beneath your conscious level?
- Do you tend to be a perfectionist, overly conscientious?
- Do you find your passion for ministry not returning after a time of vacation or rest?
- Do you have no other hobbies or diversions besides church activities?
- Do you check out ministry-job online sites frequently?
- Do you find yourself checking the Sunday attendance and the giving statistics first thing Monday morning?
- Do you find yourself coasting in ministry too often?
- Do you feel guilty when you relax?
- When you see certain people at church, is what bothers you about them the first thing that comes to mind?
- When you're with your wife or kids, do you feel not truly present with and for them?
- Has the fun factor in ministry begun to disappear?

Clueless Pastors, Clueless People

The sizeable group most at risk is those pastors who deny they have frustrations. Both the Barna Group and LifeWay surveys indicated that about one in ten pastors doesn't believe he experiences any frustrations. Really? These guys must be serving in Emerald City under names like "Pastor Oz." Another 3 percent (LifeWay) to 5 percent (Barna Group) couldn't think of any. So 12 to 15 percent of all pastors are either out of touch with reality, too proud to admit their struggles, or serve churches full of angels and leprechauns. One verbatim response summarizes this denial view: "I do not have any problems. I get along with everybody."

From the congregation's perspective, many live in that same bubble. The Barna Group survey of 650 adults who identified themselves as Christian discovered a huge disconnect between pastor and people. *Twenty-five percent* said they have no idea what might frustrate their pastor. Their apparent failure even to have considered this suggests that individualism has crept into many churches. Many come as consumers to get their needs met but don't feel responsible to invest enough to know how to help their pastors be most effective. David Kinnaman, Barna Group president, wrote in his comments: "Apparently empathy is not a characteristic of many churches."

Another common reply, given by 12 percent—about one in every eight respondents—was that *they do not believe anything about their church frustrates or disappoints their pastor.* It seems many are so self-absorbed or so disconnected from their church life that they just don't get it. Their responses imply that a pastor could (or should) lead a complex organization whose mission is to change the world and yet not experience any significant challenges in that role. In total, almost 40 percent of those we serve have no clue what frustrates us, or think nothing does. The older the congregation the greater the disconnect. The research revealed that *48 percent of those sixty-three or older have no clue what frustrates their pastors.*

The lyrics to Casting Crowns' "Slow Fade," which poignantly speak to the insidious nature of many tiny bad decisions and ignored frustrations, say that neither people, nor daddies, nor families ever crumble in a day. We might add one more line: Pastors never do either. We crumble little by little when we ignore "termites," tell ourselves *it is no big deal*, and then one day an odor shocks us awake: It is the odor of death—either of passion, our marriage, or our ministry.

The next chapter unpacks what 1,900 pastors said about what church people do that frustrates them. The answers point to these potential ministry killers. As a leader friend of mine once told me, "A thousand digs *will* bury a pastor."[30]

Questions to Ponder

1. Do you know any pastors who have been fired from a position? If so, what were the issues that led to their termination, and could they have done something to avoid it?
2. Have you experienced a time when you lost your passion for ministry? What caused it? What helped you regain it?
3. Compared to a few years ago, is ministry more difficult for you now? Why or why not?

PART II

"WHAT WE'VE GOT HERE IS . . . A FAILURE TO COMMUNICATE"

(What Almost 2,000 Pastors and More Than 600 Church Members Revealed)

CHAPTER 4

SCHOOLYARD BULLIES WHO EAT OUR LUNCH (WHAT REALLY BOTHERS US)

I know God will not give me anything I can't handle. I just wish He didn't trust me so much.

—Mother Teresa

Nerdy, wimpy, pimply, and skinny . . . apt adjectives for me as a teenager. A few summers during those awkward years I worked as a lifeguard at the local Lions Club pool. I felt so self-conscious about my large schnoz, my shoulder blades (that poked out like pectoral fins), and my ostrich legs that I'd try not to let girls get a side view of me. I appeared somewhat normal from the front, if I pushed my shoulders back. I developed excellent peripheral vision; if I noticed a cute girl look my way, I'd quickly "snap to" my best angle.

My physique gave me other problems as well: school bullies. I couldn't defend myself. I tried protein powder, weight lifting, and the ThighMaster, but I must have missed the muscle gene at conception.

As a freshman, a twice-my-size bully (I think his name was Brutus) often scared the snot out of me with his threats. Between classes one day, in a crowded hallway, I tripped him; he fell onto his brown bag lunch, flattening his bologna sandwich and Fritos. I loved it, and he didn't know I was the culprit. The experience did embolden me to believe that, if necessary, I could protect myself with some fancy footwork.

The previous year I'd faced another bully, a girl built like a refrigerator. (I think her name was Zelda—she might have been Brutus's half cousin.) For some reason, in science class one day I ticked her off, and that entire hour she stared a hole into the back of my head. Finally, with a wicked grin, she leaned over my desk, locked eyes with me, and whispered, "After class I'm going to whip your ___."

Beads of sweat formed on my forehead. I envisioned every skinny bone broken and my nose taken down two sizes (which wouldn't have been so bad). This would definitely affect my future presidency of the Junior Science Club.

I watched the wall clock as the seconds ticked down. As soon as the bell rang I bolted from the classroom, leaving a roadrunner trail of dust behind. Fortunately, my muscle deprivation didn't affect my running ability. I outpaced her, and my skeleton remained intact. I later became president of the Junior Science *and* Junior Beta Clubs (groups for nerds like me).

Most of us dealt with bullies as kids. And, whether or not we're aware, we still do. Bullies that could kill or at least break our ministries lurk in our churches.

I don't necessarily mean a bully in the sense that a board member would stalk you after church to ambush you at your car. (That usually happens *during* your monthly meetings.) Rather, I mean problems, frustrations, and irritations that come from people who rob our joy, deter our focus, and decrease our effectiveness. They can loom large or small.

Brian, a pastor in the East, tells about a bully he faced:

When I drove by the office of a long-time elder to pay him a spontaneous visit, I realized every car in the parking lot represented a trusted friend, a brother for whom I would have taken bullets. I assumed he had landed a sale and left a voice mail to congratulate him on his apparent success. It wasn't until I arrived home and mentioned the incident to my wife that I realized the cars were familiar. I soon found out that our elders were having a secret meeting to discuss my dismissal as their pastor.

For over seven years I had faithfully led this church. My sermons taught solid biblical truth, my leadership had been influenced by top pastors in the country, and my service to the body had been sacrificial. By God's grace marriages had been saved, ministries launched, and the lost had been found. Since our initial Sunday, the attendance had almost doubled and giving quadrupled.

We also completed a new state-of-the-art facility and were poised for a very bright future. But we had some challenges along the way. A satellite campus didn't pan out. People were uncomfortable with the new facility because "it didn't feel the same" as the older campus. And our new emphasis on multi-ethnic ministry, especially with Romanians, left some quarters of the church feeling neglected. I often heard, "Our pastor cares more for them than for us."

In the process, a few key staff left to find greener pastures, and a few stayed to get rid of their current pastor. I was in the midst of a staff infection. We had been infected with divisiveness. Over a shockingly short time span, men and women who I believed would be smiling at my children's weddings were engaged in malicious gossip and severe destructive criticism. Loyalty and morale eroded as a spirit of negativity engulfed my ministry. Before I knew it, I was the target of an aggressive smear campaign where my every move was interpreted in the worst possible light.

Since I'm far from perfect, they had plenty of material. Yet none of my flaws revolved around moral failure, unethical decisions, or biblical infidelity. As I look back, I still feel the deep wounds of a critical movement that took aim at my character, my calling, even my wife and children. It was appalling and terribly damaging.

God enabled us to persevere. And eventually the critics either left or experienced a change of heart. God took care of it and took care of us. Both the church and I are now more mature.

I can only imagine the pain Brian felt. As far as I know, the elders of churches where I've served never held clandestine gatherings to consider my ouster. (If they did, it's probably best I never knew.) The board questioning his leadership was a bully, a potential killer that weighed heavily on him, a weight that potentially could sink any pastor's passion.

Five Ministry Killers

Every church is different, and the bullies you face are unique to your setting. The research, however, did point to five overall potential killers most prevalent in pastors' lives. The list isn't exhaustive but reflects common threads found in churches.

1. **Head-in-the-sand mentality.** I've mentioned that a surprising percentage of pastors indicated they serve churches without problems (or are unaware of any). I don't devote a specific chapter to this issue because the solutions I suggest for the other killers apply to this one also.
2. **Misdirected emotional investment.** Many pastors place much of their emotional capital into issues upon which Scripture does not place highest value. The bulk of this chapter focuses on this killer; another chapter suggests ways to defeat it.
3. **Unhealthy responses to ministry killers.** This includes two aspects: what we do and what we don't do. On the do side, numerous pastors respond to ministry problems unproductively and even destructively. On the don't-do side, pastors generally keep their frustrations to themselves, which causes them to seldom ask others for helpful changes. I devote two chapters to the research dimension of this killer and another two to the solution facet.

4. **An attitude that "God and I can handle this."** A large percentage of pastors attempt to handle ministry stress in solitude. As a result, they don't invite into their lives safe people who could help them understand and appropriately deal with their issues. I take an entire chapter to encourage pastors to find friends who will help them walk through their valleys and defeat their ministry killers.
5. **Lonely, hurting wives.** Shockingly, pastors seldom mentioned this prominent issue. The silence led me to rank it as a top-five silent but deadly killer, especially since both my wife and I have seen its prevalence. We take a chapter to dialogue about it, and I reference other research that points to its ubiquity.

Instead of dissecting killer number one first, then number two, and so on, I've organized the remainder of the book in this way: I immediately describe what the research tells us about our frustrations in the church, how we respond to them, and what we'd like the people we serve to do differently. Thereafter I devote an entire section (Part III) to how we can defeat those killers and thus become healthier pastors, more effective leaders, and increasingly joy-filled servants for Jesus.[1]

Both the Barna Group (surveying 615 pastors) and LifeWay (1,002 pastors) posed this question:

> *Think about the challenges pastors often face when it comes to their relationships with people who attend the church. For you, what are the types of issues that cause the most disappointment or frustration between you and the people in your church?*

Each study categorized the responses into subcategories.[2] I've included the top-ten responses for both.[3]

The Barna Group Research Survey[4]

Category	Percentage
Lack of commitment in general	19%
Lack of commitment to grow spiritually/walk as Christians	15%
Congregants' lifestyle and morality struggles	13%
Lack of commitment to serve in ministry	10%
No problems	10%
Lack of commitment in church attendance	8%
Problems with communication	8%
Relationships/problems between congregants	7%
Unrealistic expectations	7%
Financial gaps and concerns	6%

LifeWay Research Survey[5]

Category	Percentage
Lack of commitment and follow-through	16%
Good situation, no problems	10%
Lack of faithfulness, inconsistent Christian living	7%
Communication, misunderstandings	6%
Don't know, not sure, not specific	5%
Lack of involvement, reluctance to participate	5%
Resistance to change, narrow-minded	4%
Absenteeism, sporadic attendance	4%
Financial issues, budget, stewardship	4%
Lack of time, busyness, schedule overload	3%

The subcategory responses were interesting enough. But since the two sets of answers resulted in similar subcategories, I was able to create super-categories I've called Mega-Themes for an approximate apples-to-apples comparison.

Three Mega-Themes

In chapter 2, I likened our frustrations to termites. The Mega-Themes extend the metaphor, because the research indicated that ministry termites seem to "colonize" into large groupings. I expected to find appreciable differences between the surveys, but to my surprise the response percentages of the Mega-Themes were almost identical. In other words, both discovered the same pastoral issues, reinforcing the findings' credibility.

I've excluded the "no frustrations/don't know" category here, as the solution to that ministry killer is rather simple: Get your head out of the sand. The following three Mega-Themes describe the areas where pastors experience the greatest frustration and, if left untended, the greatest passion-leak.

Mega-Theme	Super-Category Summary	Percentage
Issues involving people's response to my leadership and their response to the church's organizational needs	Issues related to the CHURCH	60%
Issues involving people's commitment to their walk with Jesus	Issues related to CHRIST	30%
Issues involving people's relationships with others in the church	Issues related to COMMUNITY	15%

In simple terms, two surveys taken, over a year apart, of two different large groups of pastors, discovered that the issues bothering us most fall into three broad categories.

- **Largest category: issues involving people's commitment to the local church (roughly 60 percent).** Issues that could hinder ministry growth, such as attendance, giving, volunteering, general local-church commitment, what the church expects of me as a pastor, the church's response to my leadership, and church direction. One verbatim response summarized these answers with "It is the commitment to the church that needs to increase."
- **Second-largest category: issues involving people's commitment to Christ (roughly 30 percent).** What we perceive as lack of faithfulness in people's walk with Jesus: apathy, discipleship and spiritual-growth deficiencies, sin issues, individual spiritual health, and living out faith.
- **Third-largest category: issues involving healthy community (roughly 15 percent).** Unhealthy interpersonal relationships among people in the church reflected in conflict, lack of unity, gossip, and poor communication.

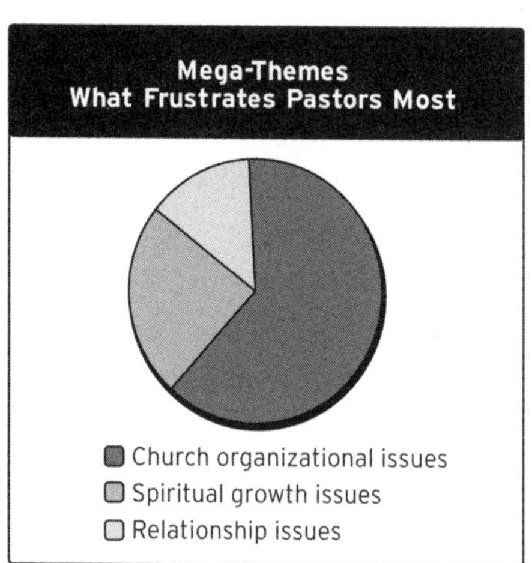

When I compared them, the Mega-Themes shocked me. *Pastors say organizational issues bother them more than issues related to the spiritual health of the people they serve, by a 2-to-1 margin. And when comparing church organizational issues to concerns about how people relate to each other, it was a 4-to-1 margin.*

Granted, the surveys didn't drill down into each

response to determine, for example, if a pastor meant to imply that a lack of volunteers was a spiritual issue in his mind rather than an organizational issue. Nor did they determine when or if frustrations about leadership/direction were meant likewise to signify spiritual factors. However, for the following reasons I believe the Mega-Themes do accurately reflect what bothers us most.

First, both surveys asked the exact same open-ended question that gave each pastor ample opportunity to answer candidly. Second, the overall results so closely aligned that we can have high confidence in the findings. Third, the surveys yielded similar subcategories that included both spiritual and organizational/leadership issues.

The research starkly indicates that what troubles us most involves what keeps our organizations from running smoothly, hinders the numerical measures of success, and causes dissonance in us when others don't want to follow our leadership. Leadership Network surveyed more than two hundred mega-church pastors in July 2009, and discovered similar results.[6]

These termites can colonize in a pastor's heart into a potent, potentially destructive force. I noticed this in an interview with a mega-church pastor in the West. When asked to name his greatest frustrations, almost every reply involved something about organization: getting people to volunteer, balancing his roles in the church, staff performance, and leading change. *Could it be that we pastors do consistently give utmost attention to organizational frustrations rather than to spiritual and relational ones?*

Alan Nelson, former executive editor of *REV Magazine*, found this to be true:

> *If I could summarize hundreds of conversations I've had with pastors the last few years, I'd say that the single biggest frustration we feel is a perceived lack of commitment in our congregations. It shows up in attendance, attitude, participation, and tithe.*[7]

What Are We Really Here For?

When I saw these Mega-Themes, it disturbed me that 60 percent of pastors seem to care more about "buildings, budgets, and numbers in the pews" than about spiritual growth or healthy relationships. But then God gently reminded me that too often I'm bothered most when things hinder church growth or don't make me look successful, feed my ego, or bolster my self-confidence.

As I wrote this chapter, I told my wife how God was convicting me that frequently in ministry I look to the wrong things to validate me. I admit it bothers me when people skip church if rain threatens but wouldn't miss their kid's soccer game if it hailed. (I like a packed auditorium when I preach.) It frustrates me when a guy won't flinch to pay a $50 green fee but balks when I teach about tithing. (The church has bills to pay too.) I don't appreciate a nitpicky comment that I didn't pronounce an Old Testament character's name correctly. (How about an occasional "Great sermon, pastor"?) It galls me when volunteers don't show up to serve in the nursery and we have to turn visitors away. (If those parents don't come back again, we lose a prospective volunteer.)

I don't mean to minimize the importance of a fully staffed nursery, the need to meet our budgets, or the dynamic created by a full house. I'm not ignoring the pain we feel when others resist our leadership. I'm not suggesting we shouldn't develop leaders, cast vision, create healthy systems, administrate well, or manage change wisely. I read several church growth and leadership books every year; I earned a degree in systems engineering and can design church systems in my sleep. All of this does matter.

However, because we pastors get sideways over organizational issues much more often than we do when our people don't live out the Great Commandment, we should start paying a different kind of attention. It appears we've skewed our priorities. And when that happens, I don't believe we'll experience the Holy Spirit's power to lead as we otherwise could.

Jesus said, " 'Love the Lord your God with all your heart and with all your soul and with all your strength and with all your mind'; and, 'Love your neighbor as yourself.' "[8] This is a clear-as-day statement of our priorities: Teach those in our church and model for them how to love God and love others above all else. When we misplace our directives, I believe we inadvertently allow ministry killers to influence us.

Bill Hull, who's written extensively on discipleship, speaks of a stark reality that hit him at age fifty. His words capture the essence of my message in this chapter:

> *Through my "dark night of the soul," I gradually realized that something was missing in my life. It was the same thing that my church growth generation has missed. I had forgotten that my life as a leader should be a reflection of my relationship to Christ. Leadership is not about competency and productivity, as we have been led to believe. Our culture values action over contemplation, individualism over community, speed over endurance, fame over humility, and success over the satisfied soul.*[9]

What most angers us, frustrates us, and bothers us reveals what's most important to us. For many pastors, including myself, even though we mentally and verbally embrace the Great Commandment (and the Great Commission), our actions too often belie our belief. As much as Jesus wanted all those who heard His message to believe and follow, His desire for true commitment trumped any desire for visible success. When He explained the cost of discipleship, His church shrank in numbers because many "no longer followed him."[10] Spiritual commitment and love for others matter more to Him than numerical success.

I'm encouraged in one way, however, in that Scripture shows this temptation to get out of balance as seeming to come with the territory. Ministry is a tough calling; the struggle is nothing new. We can't hold up contemporary technology, our ever-changing culture, Viagra, or multifaceted ministries as the culprit. *The very nature of ministry tempts us to focus on the wrong priorities.* Moses would have been toast had he not listened to his father-in-law, who advised him to delegate many administrative tasks so he could focus on the primary ones.[11]

The early church leaders also struggled to keep balance. The apostles dealt with the tension between meeting a growing congregation's pragmatic and spiritual needs. Thus they gathered the church together and appointed managerial deacons so they themselves could focus on the body's spiritual needs. Luke records this solution in Acts.

> *So the Twelve called a meeting of all the believers. They said, "We apostles should spend our time teaching the word of God, not running a food program. And so, brothers, select seven men who are well respected and are full of the Spirit and wisdom. We will give them this responsibility. Then we apostles can spend our time in prayer and teaching the word."*[12]

We should feel encouraged: We *can* achieve balance. Certainly ministry often thrusts us into CEO and CFO roles. But I believe we can fulfill them effectively without diminishing our servant-leader roles, our calling to point people to a deeper walk with Christ and to healthy relationships with one another. We must make it our priority to empower others in their spiritual journeys rather than getting them to empower us in ours.

I don't speak as an expert who has "finally arrived." I often get mired in that 60-percent category, as an incident in a recent staff meeting reminded me:

We hold two services each Sunday; one week, because attendance was undercounted for the second service, I added to the attendance figures. But one of our pastors then remarked that when he tabulated the first service he discovered it had been over-counted. Immediately I felt defensive; the prospect that attendance was up validated my leadership, yet when it looked like attendance was down, I felt invalidated.

It's so easy to look to the wrong benchmarks to feel successful. Perhaps Jesus has a lesson for us in His words to Peter:

> *You are a stumbling block to me; you do not have in mind the things of God, but the things of men.*[13]

I don't believe most pastors want organizational issues to colonize into giant bullies that drain our limited energy. We don't want misplaced priorities to become ministry killers. We only have so much to give. So why not prioritize what Jesus tells us is most important—that which will produce the most lasting fruit and real joy?

I want to be bothered more by what bothers Jesus. I want my heart to break more often over what breaks His heart: people who don't love Him or love each other well. And I believe when I align myself more with what matters *most* to Him, His Spirit will empower me to lead at my best and will sustain my joy for ministry. (In a later chapter I'll suggest a way to help us better align what frustrates us with what would frustrate Jesus if He were in our shoes.)

Communication and Connection

My wife and I usually communicate well together. We've been married long enough to know intuitively when something is bothering the other. When we sense an issue, we talk, and our conversation strengthens our relationship.

Likewise, I believe that the more a pastor and a pastor's church know each other, the stronger that relationship becomes. I sought to discover how well our churches know what frustrates us and also who gives us the greatest grief. NationalChristianPoll.com revealed interesting insights; when pastors were asked if they thought people understood their frustrations, here's how they responded:

A majority believes the people in our churches have no clue what truly bothers us. And another four out of ten believe they're only somewhat aware.

Later we'll examine the merits of communicating these issues to the church, staff, and key leaders. Imagine for a moment, though, that some things you do irritate your wife but that she never verbalizes them to you; she stuffs them inside and gets angrier each time you repeat them. Perhaps they're small. Perhaps they're large. And certainly we hope that as we grow in relationship, we all become more tolerant and overlook lots of quirks. But imagine what would happen to your relationship if all the emotion was stuffed.

For example, I'm a type-A personality, a "place for everything and everything in its place" kind of guy. In our early days I'd kid my wife that her idea of a storage place—where to lay something down—was anything with a flat surface. Let's just say she is more *flexible* than I am in that area. Fortunately I've lightened up since then. But we've often talked about issues like this, those subtle irritants. We both brought undesirable behaviors and attitudes into our marriage, and had we stuffed them, they could have become places where bitterness would fester and in turn, hurt our relationship.

I believe the same holds true for our relationship with those we serve. If 51 percent of pastors say our people probably have no clue about what they do that ticks us off, and we don't adequately process and appropriately communicate these frustrations, they *will* become destructive bullies, even ministry killers. In chapter 9, we'll delve into the Barna Group survey of more than 600 church attendees asking which of their behaviors frustrate their pastors. It's interesting to note, however, how closely the pastors' assessment mirrored the response from church attenders:

Almost four out of ten church people either had no clue about what they do that bothers their pastors, felt that pastors didn't have problems, or could not name a frustration.

Another insight from the 297 pastors in the *Christianity Today* survey is *who* frustrates us most. In response to "What group of people in your church causes you the greatest frustration and disappointment," pastors were given eight choices, including an "other" group that allowed a write-in answer. Here's how they responded:

Groups That Frustrate Pastors Most[14]

Response	Percentage
People who've been around awhile	62%
Older people	24%
Layleaders	21%
More mature Christians	17%
Younger people	5%
Newer people in the church	4%
New Christians	2%
Other/no one frustrates me	26%

Apparently longer-standing church members and older people bring more stress to pastors than do younger people and those newer to the church. I've experienced this. When I've come into a church and brought change, those members who had tenure tended to resist more than those who came after I arrived. As a close friend pointed out, the former group also has great potential for pastoral support and organizational stability if we tap into their influence. For some reason, though, we often seem to miss opportunities to enfold these committed people into the church's future.

The write-in responses below capture the general tone of the "other" category. The last two particularly struck a chord in me.

- un-Christlike Christians
- those with a personal agenda
- the joy suckers: those self-righteous, self-absorbed know-it-alls
- controlling people
- people who aren't happy with their own lives
- non-Christ-follower Christians
- people who see church as their personal ATM

This chapter has described three primary issues that frustrate us most: church organizational challenges, weak spiritual formation among those we serve, and unhealthy relationships among those same people. I've stated that apparently we give those real and pressing organizational matters too much of our limited time and energy; our priorities seem out of whack. When that happens, our focus and attention on Great Commandment and Great Commission priorities becomes diluted and we more easily lose our joy.

In chapter 8, I'll suggest ways we can reprioritize.

Also, we've seen that many who attend our churches don't know what stresses us and that we believe the majority is clueless. In chapter 10, we'll walk through a process to discover with whom you need to communicate.

Now, in chapter 5, we'll unpack research that discovered how we actually, currently respond to these ministry bullies.

Questions to Ponder

1. Do any of the "five ministry killers" resonate with you? If not any of those, what immediately comes to mind that could be a killer for you?
2. Were you surprised at the large percentage of responses indicating that church organization issues top the list of pastoral frustrations? How prevalent would you say this is among the pastors you know?
3. Do you agree that we should direct our greatest energy toward the Great Commandment? Why or why not?

CHAPTER 5

PUNCH 'EM OUT, TELL THE TEACHER, OR SKIP LUNCH? (HOW WE RESPOND)

I don't think pastors "burn out" because they work too hard. People who work hard often do so because they're good at what they're doing and they enjoy doing it. I think burnout comes from working with no relational gratification.[1]

—Eugene H. Peterson

Pastor John had just finished his final message as the second service concluded. With a weary "pastor's grin" on his face, he chatted with those who lingered. He was exhausted, ready to go home for a well-deserved nap. Just as he grabbed his Bible to leave, two women approached—one he knew was never happy and the other a supportive member who looked rather sheepish. The latter began the conversation with "Pastor, Ann here wants to tell you something that happened this past week."

He thought, *Wonderful, just what I need, another disgruntled member.* With a disingenuous caring tone he asked, "What happened?" As the veins in Ann's neck swelled she blurted, "I want you to know that I left three voice mails with the youth minister to talk to him about a problem I'm having with my son. And he never called me back. That so-called *youth minister* of yours is not doing his job. My son needed help, and he didn't even care enough to call me back."

As John's face flushed, he slowly responded, "Ann, I'm sure Pastor Jimmy tried to call you back and wasn't able to reach you. I will check with him and have him call you again tomorrow. I'm very sorry the two of you didn't connect."

She retorted, "Well, I've decided I'm going to another church where the pastors care about people." To punctuate her statement, she crossed her arms and stood up straight with a what-do-you-think-about-that stare.

Masking his desire to karate chop her larynx, he cleared his throat and answered, "Okay, Ann, I understand your concern, and you must do what you feel is best for your family. But I will get to the bottom of this."

She then spun around and stormed off; her friend grimaced and followed like a whipped puppy. John's nap that afternoon wasn't so restful. For several days he mulled over this encounter and kept his pain to himself, even after discovering that his youth pastor had indeed attempted to contact Ann.

The worst was yet to come. Two weeks later he received a call from a woman with whom he'd often faced conflict. She had shown herself to be quite the drama queen, and her family was the church's biggest giver. She requested a meeting to "discuss an issue."

She and her husband arrived at his office, and after a few pleasantries she explained that Ann had called her about the recent conversation. Ann was "very upset" because he "hadn't been responsive to her need." John tried to explain what happened from his perspective, but her mind was made up. Then with dramatic flair, she swept her arms outward, and her voice quivered as she said, "Why didn't you just reach out your arms and give her a big hug?" As John's puke level rose to Orange, he didn't know what to say except "I'm sorry she felt the way she did." This ended the conversation. (A few months later that couple also felt "led of the Holy Spirit" to look for a new church home.)

As John sat in his office chair that night his emotions roiled. After he breathed a short prayer he went home. His wife asked how his day went, and he replied with a less-than-forthright "Okay, nothing much out of the ordinary." He didn't want to burden her—she too had often endured the ire of the drama queen. He wished he knew someone with whom to process his pain. For the next two weeks he spent the bulk of his quiet time praying about this disappointment.

John's story illustrates what the research discovered to be one of the two most common ways pastors handle these issues—by ourselves and in prayer. We all unconsciously turn to our default responses when we face ministry bullies. However, often those instincts alone aren't healthy, or at best are one-sided. Harboring pain privately can become a ministry killer.

I can trace my typical response to ministry frustration to the way I reacted to bullies. The high school I attended in Georgia began with the eighth grade. One day during my first year a buddy and I were in the bathroom just before our next class began. I carried my books in a Samsonite-sized briefcase. Two upperclassmen, looking for trouble, walked in and noticed the case.

I hoped they were going to think it belonged to my friend, but my pocket protector must have given me away. They began to chide me; it looked like they were going to rough me up. As they began their move, I feigned madness, literally. I began to talk like a cartoon character (Daffy Duck, I think) and bugged out my eyes like I was insane. I guess I subconsciously remembered a VBS lesson about King David doing something similar.[2] Well, it worked! The bullies looked at each other and mumbled, "This guy is nuts. Let's get out of here." I avoided a bloody nose that day.

My default response to bullies and conflict? *Avoidance.* I'd do anything to sidestep a bully's ire, by any means from running to pretending. Some pastors tend to handle their issues in the same way.

The Barna Group research probed what we do in response to our frustrations and disappointments with this question: *Think back to the last time you felt disappointed or frustrated with people in your congregation. What did you do—if anything—to address the challenges you faced?* The pastors could mention anything that came to mind. Here are the top ten responses:[3]

Response	Percentage
Prayed about the issue	37%
Confronted the issue immediately	34%
Had someone on ministry team/board/staff deal with the issue	15%
Looked for Scripture to address, solve the problem	14%
Sought counsel from someone I trusted	10%
Talked with the person	9%
Confronted the issue eventually	9%
Addressed it from the pulpit/in a sermon	4%
Had a council meeting/board meeting	2%
Self-examination	2%

Survey research in general shows how people want to be perceived and may not always reflect an objective reality. Nevertheless, this provides a snapshot of *how pastors perceive themselves responding to issues.*

The first two choices, prayer and immediate confrontation, were mentioned almost equally. These and the other responses raised interesting observations. I've used animal characteristics below to highlight them (but please don't press the metaphors too far).

The Sloth: Stay Detached

Several years ago I took our family to Georgia's Callaway Gardens to visit the Day Butterfly Center. In a large, temperature-controlled glass building visitors can walk along paths inside to enjoy butterflies that fly around freely and even land on people. I enjoyed our excursion, but what interested me most was the challenge given by one of the guides: "Look up in the trees and see if you can find the sloth." After half an hour, I finally spotted him clinging to a branch about twenty feet above my head. A placard explained that sloths rarely move and only come down to poop. "Passive, detached, and unaware" best describes them.

Some pastors respond similarly to ministry frustration. In the survey, when added together, the categories "did nothing," "no problems/disappointments," and "not sure" equaled 13 percent. Among pastors, more than one in ten defaults to an unhealthy disregard for—or detachment from—a potential ministry killer. If you're in this group, I hope you'll carefully read chapter 8 (where I suggest that we all must own up to our responses to frustrations, even if we deny we have any).

The Skunk: Leave the Mess to Others

Our offices are located in a corner of our church building. A side door allows us to bypass the main entrance. One morning, arriving around eight, I parked my Nissan truck about fifty feet from the door and began walking. About ten feet from the building, I peripherally noticed movement to my left and at first thought it was a cat. I stopped dead in my tracks when I saw that it actually was a full-grown skunk that noticed me too.

He also froze in his tracks and slowly lifted his tail as our eyes locked. As I edged away I claimed the promise of Psalm 91:10—"There shall no evil befall thee, neither shall any plague come nigh thy dwelling."[4] Maybe I didn't *exactly* quote that, but I sure was namin', claimin', and prayin' like I hadn't done in quite a while. After the skunk saw I was giving him his space, he sauntered off without incident.

Had God not answered my prayer (or had I not simply moved back), the sprayed skunk scent would have made me a very unpopular pastor for a few days. Again, don't press the image too far, but some pastors respond to their frustrations by handing off their stinky issues to somebody else (see the third largest category, above, at 15 percent). Certainly in some cases we *should* delegate problems to others. But I wonder if sometimes we delegate to avoid uncomfortable conflict we rightfully should face ourselves. When we do, we truly are missing opportunities God is giving us to grow.

The Hawk: Look Through a Window, Not in a Mirror

On my way to the gym each day I drive by a large open field. Often I see a hawk perched on a telephone pole, staring out into that field. I'm no ornithologist, but I know hawks have keen eyesight and love mice for snacks. They constantly look for unsuspecting prey.

One tiny statistic revealed a most disconcerting discovery. Down the list of responses to ministry frustrations, number ten was "self-examination." Only two out of a hundred pastors responded to their frustrations by looking at themselves as contributing to the problem. Like the hawk, many of us keenly look outward toward others but don't peer inward to see how we may be complicit in our struggles.

David Kinnaman observed in his written comments on the Barna Group research:

> *Leaders exhibit very limited capacity or willingness to self-examine. This is not entirely unexpected; it's human nature. Yet pastors rarely suggested that they look inward as part of their solution to challenges. Virtually none of the 615 leaders we interviewed said that their frustration or disappointment is that they can't lead their people better—or considered that the commitment vacuum displayed by their congregants might somehow be a reflection of inadequate leadership.*

This reminded me of an insight taught by Jim Collins, who uses a mirror and a window as metaphors to teach a quality great leaders exhibit.

Superb leaders don't look out the window to blame others. They look in a mirror to take ownership when things don't go well and look out a window to praise others when things do go well.

The rarity and paucity of self-examination should cause us to take inventory of our responsibility in church friction. Ignoring this could easily become a ministry killer as others begin to see us either as blamers or as shirkers.

The Turtle: Hide Behind Spirituality

I love turtles, especially box turtles. I've probably saved half a dozen from getting pancaked when I've pulled over and jumped out of my car to rescue one ambling across a road. I even kept a pet box turtle in my backyard when I was forty years old. I used the excuse that it was my son's.

Any kid who's ever had a box turtle knows what it does when you pick it up: It instantly pulls its head and legs into its shell to hide. In similar fashion, sometimes we pastors duck our frustration by retreating into our spiritual shells. At first blush, the 37 percent who prayed about their frustrations look quite spiritual. But I wonder how often prayer becomes an excuse to avoid dealing with issues at hand. When "pray about the issue" is combined with "look for Scripture to address/solve the problem," the percentage jumps to over 50 percent who choose private spiritual means as their default response.

I laud pastors who do this. However, a deeper look reveals something else. The Barna Group's written analysis of the data noted:

> *The clear picture that emerges from this is that pastors generally solve problems with one extreme or another—either through "human" effort to confront the problem, or through "super-spiritualizing" the issue—but rarely through both. Many pastors "hide" behind prayer. . . .*

The Lion: I'm Quite Comfortable in My Own Skin

We give lions an honored position: "King of the Jungle." I understand why; I've had a lot of experience with the behavior of lions. Well, I watch Discovery Channel, and I saw *Lion King* twice. Although I've never personally encountered one, I know lions roar a lot, exude self-confidence, lie around a bunch, and usually get their way. As a leader I hope I exude appropriate self-confidence. And I do like getting my way.

Over a third of the pastors indicated that when faced with frustration they immediately confront the issue. Although some issues do warrant a quick, self-confident response, many should lead to a more thoughtful and deliberate approach. Unfortunately, we may over-lean on our strength, as the researcher's written analysis noted. "Many pastors . . . are a little too comfortable in their skin, without relying on prayer and self-examination to give spiritual context to their confrontations."

Although I tend to be a turtle by handling my hurt in private and in prayer, I've also roared too quickly at someone who ticked me off. Too often I've verbally fired back in defensiveness at someone who criticized me, or shot back an instant e-mail only to regret it later. Moses, reacting in anger to the mistreatment of his people, murdered an Egyptian, and then looked over his shoulder for the next forty years.

Healthy Balance Between Lion and Turtle?

Since the research indicates most of us respond to frustration with one of two extremes, can we achieve a healthy balance? Can we avoid allowing our responses to become ministry killers? Granted, it's tough to respond appropriately in the moment. Sometimes we should just pull away, pray, and believe that love *will* cover a multitude of sins.[5] But prayer should never become an excuse to shirk conflict, and sometimes we must quickly confront an issue before it gets out of control. Plus, if we're *too* quick we may miss the gentle voice of God's Spirit tempering our response.

The Barna Group's written analysis also observed:

> *A surprisingly small [percentage] said they both prayed and confronted the problem right away—a dual-pronged approach that was identified by just 11 percent of pastors. Even if we are generous in our definition and include any pastor who confronted the problem eventually or "talked with the person," only 14 percent of all pastors said they did this type of face-to-face interaction along with prayer.*

Kinnaman summarized well this tension between the lion and turtle responses:

> *Prayer is great, but is it a means to hear from the Holy Spirit or a way to delay a decision or a confrontation? I think it's interesting that many pastors are likely to suggest passive or even passive aggressive methods of dealing with interpersonal problems. And many of those who say they confront something immediately, do so without prayer, Scripture guidance, or input from advisors. In other words, few pastors follow a biblical process of dealing with conflict.*

I don't want to unduly criticize pastors. I hope this book will encourage pastors. Probably no other vocation places a greater expectation on a leader to balance confrontation and self-confidence with spiritual restraint and humility. We're under constant scrutiny. Intentionally or unintentionally, people develop higher standards for us than they do for themselves. Often they expect us to be faultless, yet we know we can never perfectly handle our disappointment and frustration.

Ministry tension comes with the territory and will never go away this side of heaven. What bothers us and how we respond should clue us in to what saps our joy and energy. If we want to stay healthy and productive for the long haul, we must pay close attention to how we respond, take full responsibility when we err, and seek to always honor Christ.

I take great comfort in that God has filled Scripture with men and women who made a great impact for Him yet were jars of clay, cracked pots with imperfections, often poorly responding to life's stresses. Both Paul and Moses murdered. Peter was a coward. David was an adulterer. Rahab was a prostitute. Matthew was a treacherous tax collector. The apostles were of "little faith."

The Bible does not conceal their character cracks, yet all of these ultimately evidenced humble, teachable, and repentant hearts. Despite their failures and disappointments, they grew in their walk with God. I hope that as we pastors become more aware of how we respond to ministry frustration and lean more and more into Christ, we will stay strong in Him and finish well.

The week I wrote this chapter, we were visiting Sherryl's dad and sister. Our vacation crossed over into Sunday, and my sister-in-law's church asked me to speak in their service. Beforehand, I chatted with the associate pastor, who told me about his ministry journey; he'd gone there after serving seventeen years in his previous church.

The next thing he mentioned stirred me deeply. He said his previous church's current pastor was now eighty and had served there for forty years. For days I couldn't shake the image of this faithful man who had so long persevered. I hope we not only will aspire to serve God for the long haul but also will emulate those who do. Healthy frustration management is crucial to that longevity, and it will help us defeat potential ministry killers.

In this chapter we examined common pastoral responses to ministry frustration, noting two extremes and several other common reactions. In chapter 9, we'll self-evaluate and develop a plan to respond in the healthiest way. Next, in chapter 6, we'll consider research that uncovered what we'd specifically like our church to do differently to make ministry more joy-filled.

Questions to Ponder

1. The last time someone confronted you after a service, how did you respond? Do you believe God was pleased with that response? Why or why not?
2. Did you see yourself in any of the animal descriptions I gave? Which one comes closest to describing you, and why?

CHAPTER 6

ENJOYING LUNCH EVEN WHEN THE BULLIES ABOUND (WHAT WE WANT FROM THOSE WE SERVE)

> *There is little praise and much criticism in the church today, and who can live for long in such a climate without slipping into some type of depression?*[1]
>
> —Henri Nouwen

I don't intend for this book to become a Bible study on leadership. I don't want to lecture, and I certainly don't want to preach. However, I'd like to spend some time on a verse that speaks to something every pastor needs to avoid to defeat ministry killers. We need it for emotional health, for sustained ministry passion, and for effective leadership.

If you're like me, some Scriptures are harder to teach than others. First Corinthians 13 is great for a series on love, a safe subject. John 15, about abiding in Christ, can provide an excellent object lesson. I can easily craft a practical message on the tongue from James 3. But have you ever tried to delicately deal with something like *Wives, submit to your husbands*, in Ephesians 5? Sherryl serves on our teaching team, and I always let her handle that one (just kidding . . . mostly).

How about "as in all the congregations of the saints, women should remain silent in the churches. They are not allowed to speak, but must be in submission" from 1 Corinthians 14?[2] The Judges 15 story of Samson killing a thousand men with a bone can test us in a subculture averse to violence. In moments of weakness, I admit I sometimes hope I can find a paraphrase to get me out of trouble with a more palatable rendering.

Of all the tough sections, teaching this one, Hebrews 13:17, on church leadership, may pose the highest challenge:

> *Obey your leaders and submit to their authority. They keep watch over you as men who must give an account. Obey them so that their work will be a joy, not a burden, for that would be of no advantage to you.*

The Message puts it this way:

> *Be responsive to your pastoral leaders. Listen to their counsel. They are alert to the condition of your lives and work under the strict supervision of God. Contribute to the joy of their leadership, not its drudgery. Why would you want to make things harder for them?*

"Obey your leaders" sounds quite strong. Certainly this does not condone dictatorial leadership, as Peter makes clear when he says, "Don't lord it over the people assigned to your care, but lead them by your good example."[3] After all, God calls us shepherds, and shepherds don't push—they lead. Unfortunately, in our world, where self is king and where those in spiritual authority have abused their power, many in our churches would struggle with a sermon titled "Obey Your Leaders."

But that's not the part upon which I want to focus. It's the last part: "that their work will be a joy, not a burden, for that would be of no advantage to you." Often it seems ministry brings more burdens than joy. After a tough meeting, I sometimes wish I could get away with giving an elder a swirly. Other times, in response to a critic, I'm tempted to use King David's words as a club: "Do not touch my anointed ones; do my prophets no harm."[4]

Other translations render "that their work will be a joy" (Hebrews 13:17) in these ways:

> *Don't make them sad as they do their work. Make them happy.* (CEV)
>
> *Let them do this with joy and not with grief.* (NASB)
>
> *Give them reason to do this joyfully and not with sorrow.* (NLT)
>
> *Let them do all this with joy and not with groaning.* (ESV)

A similar verse mirrors this one. Paul writes,

> *We ask you, brothers, to respect those who work hard among you, who are over you in the Lord and who admonish you.*[5]

Other translators render *respect* (Greek: *oida*) as "appreciate" (NASB), "be thoughtful of" (CEV), "honor" (THE MESSAGE, NLT), and "pay proper respect to" (TEV). On the other hand, just as "obey your leaders" can sound dictatorial, these statements can sound like they promote the self-serving, egotistical, and narcissistic.

Don't make us sad.
Honor us.
Respect us.
Make us happy.
Appreciate us.
Give us reasons to be joyful.

These thoughts likewise might seem oxymoronic when contrasted to our ministerial call to selflessly give ourselves away. But no matter how they're translated, these verses raise some important questions. Is it wrong to want our ministries to bring us joy? Could it be called a sin—or at best self-serving—to expect from our congregation certain behaviors that would make our serving them more joyful and less burdensome?

Should we dare even broach these matters? Did one pastor correctly assess church folk when he said, "Most truly aren't concerned with my joy"? Conversely, should we affirm the answer of several others that "My joy is from the Lord, not from people"?

I don't suggest a simplistic solution to pastoral joy. However, God's Word leaves no room for misunderstanding. He expects believers to respond to healthy pastoral leadership by taking concrete steps to help make ministry more fulfilling for His servants.

I've used the bully metaphor to describe our frustrations and ministry killers. These "bullies" will never disappear. We lead sheep, and sheep get messy. But *God* has planted certain desires in our hearts that when met help ameliorate the unavoidable stress and pain ministry brings. As we serve those in our church, and they serve us in ways that bring us joy, our frustrations *will* become easier to bear.

Giving Versus Taking

Let's examine Hebrews 13:17 a bit more. The writer says Christians should follow, respect, and honor their pastors. When they do, both pastor and people benefit.

The pastor experiences more joy that in turn energizes him to serve and lead more effectively. The imagery in the original language describes a pastor's heart, picturing someone who keeps awake at night out of concern for the spiritual welfare of another. Our diligence to serve and lead is reinforced by God's expectation that we must give an account of our ministry.

The people also benefit, inferred by the word *advantage*. When too many burdens come from those we serve, the weight can dilute our passion and strength to serve. Thus, there is no *advantage* to them. *Burden* (what happens in ministry with no joy) describes a deep inner groaning, something every pastor has experienced when things go awry.

Although we can't demand that others bring us joy, through our actions and attitude we can create an environment that encourages it to happen. I believe we create this joy-inviting atmosphere when we align what frustrates us with what frustrates God's heart. When our concerns align with His, the Spirit gives us His joy to deal with them.

Hebrews 13:17 suggests a clue as to how this atmosphere affects us. *Perseverance in the faith* runs through Hebrews as a major motif, one that indicates what *advantage* might mean (translated *profit* in the NASB). When believers make choices that give us joy, we get energized, which in turn helps us focus on what helps them persevere (grow) in their faith, which encourages their positive response to our leadership. Let's call this the Mutual *Giving* Cycle.

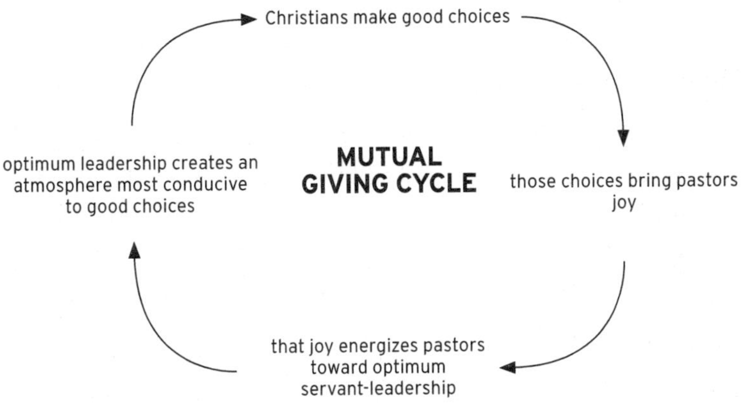

In contrast, the opposite occurs when church people make choices that burden us. I've called this process the Mutual *Taking* Cycle.

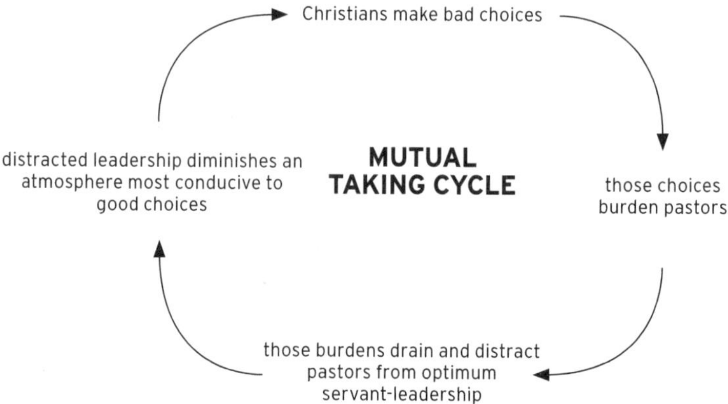

This concept does raise a form of the chicken-and-egg question: Should pastors create the atmosphere, and then people respond to it, or should people do the things that bring us joy so that in turn we pastors receive the energy to create the atmosphere? Although it's a both/and issue, pastors should take the lead and apply Romans 15:1:

> *Those of us who are strong and able in the faith need to step in and lend a hand to those who falter, and not just do what is most convenient for us. Strength is for service, not status.*[6]

Again, our desire for joy in ministry isn't self-serving, although if taken too far it could be. Responding to good pastoral leadership in ways that bring joy to pastors is biblical. We help create this Mutual Giving Cycle when those in our churches truly feel we have their best interests in mind (e.g., spiritual and relational health) versus subtly communicating to them that ministry is all about us (e.g., attend and give and don't ever question my leadership). It's an application of the principle "People don't care how much you know until they know how much you care."

I must mention one caveat, however. Throughout Scripture God reminds us that pain and disappointment can be powerful catalysts for change. And contentment may even stagnate us if we seek to maintain it at the cost of personal growth. *Even when those we serve make life miserable for us, God will mature and grow us if we let Him.* So our ultimate goal always must be Christlikeness, whether it comes through pain (incessant frustrations) or blessing (choices by those we serve that bring us joy).

Perhaps an example will help contrast the Giving and Taking Cycles. Several years ago a woman in the church I served sent an e-mail asking to meet with me. When trouble is brewing, we often have a sixth sense forewarning us that a pending meeting is about some unmet expectation or church problem. Well, it took a few weeks for us to connect, but the issue had already been telegraphed to me.

I had scheduled a feedback session with several members who helped me craft some themes for an upcoming series. Just as we were about to finish, one guy spoke up: "I hope this series will be a lot deeper than the recent sermons. My small group has extensively discussed them, and we all agree that we've been getting a lot of fluff lately." At that moment ungodly thoughts leaped into my mind. However, I mustered a fake preacher smile to convey, "That kick to the groin didn't hurt one bit. Kick me again. I am Pastor. I am strong."

The next day I discovered this man's group leader was the woman who requested the meeting. We finally met for a frank and positive discussion. She's still in the church, but I'm not sure about those in her group. That experience sucked some life out of me and illustrates how church people can contribute to the Mutual Taking Cycle.

Ironically, this same woman caught me one day between services and complimented me on my preaching. I had just completed a series on spiritual disciplines, and one message was on fasting. She said my message had connected so well with her that she later fasted for the first time. I felt encouraged and energized, which helped contribute to the

Mutual Giving Cycle. Positive deposits through specific actions from those we serve clearly bring us joy.

What Do We Really Want?

Previously I summarized a research discovery: Pastors indicated that church organizational issues bothered them more than issues related to people's spiritual health by 2 to 1. And when comparing organizational issues to their concerns about how people treat each other, it was 4 to 1. Both statistics potentially indicate out-of-balance priorities. While not denying that church organization and directional issues affect us, I contend that Jesus would want our energies most expended on the spiritual and relational ones. When pragmatic ministry responsibilities trump spiritual and relational concerns, we potentially invite a ministry killer into our lives.

However, if we regularly communicate our frustration when people don't attend, give, volunteer, or follow, they can sense a self-serving attitude within us. The research indicates that many times we do intentionally or unintentionally communicate such a message. Granted, our encouragement of things like attendance and volunteering doesn't always indicate a self-serving motive. But the surveys clearly suggest that the message sent from us *and* the one heard by church people is that we're most troubled when they don't contribute to organizational success.

In late 2008, the Barna Group surveyed over 1,000 people, of which 650 identified themselves as Christians. They posed this question:

> *Some pastors experience frustration or disappointment with the people who attend the church they pastor. Thinking about the church you attend most often, what is it about the people or that congregation that is most likely to cause frustration or disappointment for the senior pastor of the church?*

The researchers clumped the answers into seventeen categories; I combined these into categories similar to the pastoral-frustration responses from the other two pastor surveys. This chart compares the answers, and here a clear picture emerges as to people's perceptions of what frustrates us most.[7]

Pastors' Greatest Frustrations[8]

Theme	Pastors Said[9]	Pastors Said[10]	People Said[11]
1. Church commitment issues	43%	38%	44%
2. Christian walk issues	28%	30%	29%
3. Leadership/directional issues	19%	18%	6%
4. Relational issues	15%	15%	9%
5. No frustrations/don't know	13%	14%	38%

Surprisingly, the percentage of people who thought church commitment issues are a pastor's biggest frustration (about four in ten) was nearly the same as what pastors said. *Whether or not we intend to convey this message, we do.* Those we serve sense that we're not pleased with their giving, volunteering, and attendance. Again, I'm not implying that these issues lack importance or that we shouldn't address them in appropriate ways. But I don't believe we can foster the Mutual Giving Cycle when we communicate that we care more about the organization than we do about relational or spiritual issues.

An atmosphere that creates positive mutuality will only occur when our teaching, communication, and lifestyle telegraphs, "I care more about your walk with Christ and your relationships with others than about anything else." When those we serve believe their spiritual interests motivate us most, I'm convinced we will see more of the organizational responses we desire (such as increased attendance and giving).

H. B. London, who serves as vice-president of Church and Clergy for Focus on the Family, authored *Pastors at Greater Risk*,[12] a book I highly recommend. His thoughts[13] capture what every pastor should make his priority:

> *As a pastor and now as a pastor to pastors . . . it has been my privilege to serve the body of Christ for 47 years. They for the most part have been blessed and productive years. Not free of challenge, but certainly ordained of the Lord.*
>
> *I have thought for many years now that my greatest frustration had nothing to do with church attendance, building projects, or financial issues. By far my greatest frustration was to see the apathy of a great percentage of the congregation who for some reason never understood their role as a "royal priesthood" . . . "a chosen people, a holy nation, a people belonging to God, that you may declare the praises of him who called you out of darkness into his wonderful light" (1 Peter 2:9).*
>
> *It hurt me to see them robbed of so many blessings.*
>
> *The other area of frustration is much the same but different in that so many were content to stay as "baby Christians" rather than grow into maturity. They could have saved themselves so much turmoil had they taken solid food rather than "living on milk." "But solid food is for the mature, who by constant use have trained themselves to distinguish good from evil" (Hebrews 5:14).*
>
> *As a pastor I never gave up on the people God had allowed me to shepherd, but so often because of immaturity or the willingness to "die daily" to the guidance of the Holy Spirit, they became closed to real truth and in some cases simply wandered away.*

So what *do* we want those in our churches to do differently? What do we believe will make ministry more fulfilling and more joy-filled? We've already seen that Christians should respect, honor, and find ways to bring joy to those who serve them. Later we'll also examine the sticky issue of how we should communicate our desires to others and to whom. But for now let's look at the research results.

While both LifeWay and NationalChristianPoll.com sought to answer the questions above, LifeWay's survey elicited a corporate, big-picture response with this question:

> *Please briefly describe what the people in your church could do differently to make your ministry in your church more joyful for you.*

The surveyors grouped the pastors' replies into fifty-two categories. I was then able to further group them into three major themes that closely parallel the three Mega-Themes (what pastors said frustrates them most).[14]

What Pastors Want Church People to Do Differently[15]

Themes: What We Want to Be Different	Percentages
1. Participate more/follow my leadership better	56%
2. Grow up spiritually	32%
3. Get along better with others	5%

The largest response implies that more than half believe they will be happier if church people participate more through (for example) attending, volunteering, giving, and responding to leadership—in other words, organizational issues. Probably culture's emphasis on our identity being based on successful performance plays into this answer, which was almost twice as common as a belief that our people's spiritual growth would bring us increased joy.

Granted, some "participate more" responses could refer to people *growing up spiritually* through volunteering or attending Sunday school. But in most cases the categories and answers were specific enough to delineate between the themes.

The most surprising statistics came from two categories within the "grow up spiritually" theme. *Only 3 percent* stated that people personally engaging the Bible more would increase joy in ministry. The same was abysmally true for prayer. Apparently we don't rank increased prayer and Bible study among our flock as keys to pastoral joy.

However, Willow Creek Community Church's widely cited Reveal study of hundreds of churches indicated that Christians want spiritual challenge. That survey also revealed that Bible reading is one of the most crucial ways to build spiritual vibrancy and satisfaction. A large percentage of believers *don't* feel spiritually challenged, and many teeter on the edge of leaving our churches.

What are we to make of the results? Let's start with an apples-to-apples comparison of pastors' self-revealed greatest frustrations to what church people perceived were our greatest frustrations. The chart below also compares the Mega-Themes of *what frustrates us* with the comparable themes of *what we'd like to be different*. The far right column incorporates the data from the chart above.

What Frustrates Pastors Versus What We Want to Be Different[16]

Mega-Theme: What Frustrates Pastors Most	What Pastors Said Frustrates Them[17]	What Church People Said Frustrates Pastors[18]	What Pastors Want to Be Different[19]
1. Church organizational issues	62%	50%	Participate more 56%
2. Spiritual growth issues	28%	29%	Grow up spiritually 32%
3. Relational issues	15%	9%	Get along with others better 5%

In the top two categories, church organization and spiritual growth, what we want to be different closely mirrors what frustrates us. About the same percentage of church people responded with similar answers. We believe we'd be happier if those we serve would participate more and become more spiritually mature. However, *it seems we don't believe that if church people got along better, we'd enjoy ministry more.* I found this surprising, since interpersonal conflict is one of the most draining issues we face.

Theoretical Versus Actual

LifeWay asked what we'd like to be different *in the future*. In contrast, Christianity Today's online survey asked for a backward look and evoked more personal answers:

> *Think about what people in your church have done for you that has personally encouraged and affirmed you as a pastor. Briefly describe the experience you would say affirmed you the most.*

These personal responses reflect heartfelt desires. Pastors, 255 of them, gave 362 responses. I then combined the research's thirteen categories into eight themes.

What Pastors Said Church People Did That Affirmed Them[20]

Theme	Percentage
1. You showed me tangible appreciation	46
notes, calls, cards, e-mails	28
monetary gifts, trips, help with expenses	9
clergy appreciation week/month	5
celebration/surprise events	4

2. *You let me know that I spiritually impacted your life*	18
told me my sermons impacted you	8
I saw spiritual growth in you	6
told me I've made a difference in your life	4
3. *You prayed for me*	8
4. *You accepted and understood me, cared for me, were there when I needed you, were sincere and honest, were a true friend*	7
5. *Other/miscellaneous*	8
6. *You supported my leadership, defended me, trusted me*	6
7. *You ministered to my wife and/or family*	4
8. *You participated, served, took your role seriously*	4

In contrast to the macro answers from the LifeWay survey, here is a micro snapshot into the heart of pastors. This poll asked what people in the church *had done* that had affirmed them, whereas LifeWay asked what people *could do* differently. When pastors answered what people could do, their number one response was "participate more," at 56 percent. However, when asked about actual affirming experiences, that category fell dead last, at only 4 percent. And the number one theme response, at 46 percent: *being appreciated with such gestures as a call or a note.*

Apparently what we think will bring us more joy (organizational participation) does not match what our experience tells us has brought more joy (encouragement from others). Clearly, small acts of kindness make the greatest deposits into the pastor's heart. Focus on the Family's 2009 survey, which also reinforced this discovery, found that "a simple expression of appreciation periodically" from their boards would demonstrate how much they're valued as pastors.[21]

Dr. David Uth, pastor of First Baptist Church in Orlando, told me that "many people [incorrectly] think we get truckloads of encouragement."[22] He then described two instances in which someone went out of the way to communicate how much he's appreciated.

The day before I edited this section, I received an encouraging e-mail from the then fiancée of one of our staff (they're now married). Here's how she ended it, making my day.

> *Charles, I don't tell you near enough, but I am often brought to tears during services at Ginger. And I grew up in the church, know the Bible, have a strong relationship with Christ, etc. I am still challenged and encouraged each Sunday. Zach jokes that he judges how good a service was by how many times I cry. :)*
>
> *Thank you for all you do, and for always trying to improve. It's a marathon and we all need to keep that perspective!*
>
> *Jacki*

Responses From the Heart

When I received both the LifeWay and NationalChristianPoll.com data, I wondered why the two surveys showed such different results. Here's what I concluded. For one thing, the latter (from Christianity Today) was not a scientific sample of pastors but rather a group of pastors who volunteered to take an occasional survey. The slightly different wording, *what affirmed you* versus *what could bring you joy,* probably influenced the replies. In addition, the online survey removed the potential fear of embarrassment that responding to a live person might cause. We often find vulnerability difficult; it's easier to write something personal anonymously than (for example) to tell it to a stranger on the phone.

I've included several answers that give additional glimpses into what encourages a pastor's heart.

- *Defending me when someone attacks me verbally.*
- *Commenting on their understanding of my challenges.*

- *When handwritten notes come from godly people they mean so much.*
- *I think the greatest affirmation I receive is when my congregation trusts me.*
- *I would say it would be the time I received a homemade card from someone in the church telling me how much she appreciated me and that she was praying for me.*
- *These words of encouragement are priceless.*
- *I don't feel like I always have to be right, but I do like to have the opportunity to express my own views. Those who are most receptive to this are very affirming.*
- *Asking me how they can pray for me. I'm not talking about the hurried, polite questions that may come on a hectic Sunday morning, but when they genuinely ask.*
- *The ministry of presence, like when they sat with me in the hospital when my wife had emergency surgery.*
- *When people go out of their way to really inquire how I'm doing.*
- *Anything not related to Sunday. I get a lot of "Great message, Pastor," but I don't know if it's sincere. A phone call a few days later that refers to something I did affirms me.*
- *The occasional person who tells me that "so and so" spoke kindly about me.*
- *When I know I have the support of my leadership.*
- *Those who know there is a spiritual and emotional cost to being a pastor even if they don't really understand.*
- *They have come into my life and family and done something totally unexpected, unexplainable, and absolutely needed (came and cleaned our house when we were sick, fixed a meal for us when times were tough, etc.).*
- *When a person takes the time to pay attention to the emotions I experience and conveys their desire to stand in prayer with me on issues that are troubling.*

When a pastor faithfully serves and seldom receives encouragement from his church, his soul and passion often wither and die. This is the saddest response I received:

> *Most think the pastor needs no encouragement or affirmation, but think that we should always be aware of his or her need for encouragement and affirmation. In thirty years of pastoring, I would say that no more than a dozen times have people shown awareness.*

In the last three chapters we've looked at ministry killers from different angles. We discovered what almost 2,000 pastors told us about what church people do that bothers us, how we respond to our frustrations, and what choices from church people we believe would make ministry more fulfilling.

The next section, part III, answers the "So what?" question. Since every pastor will continue to face potential ministry killers, what can we learn from this research to help us defeat them? *The diagram illustrates the four key decisions I believe we must make to keep our passion and emotional health vibrant.*

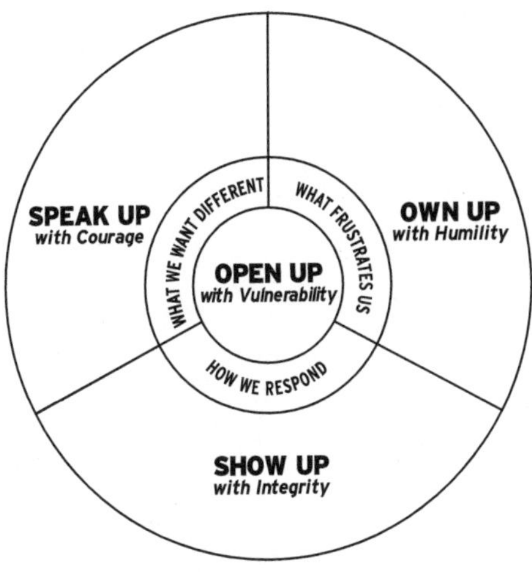

The next chapter, which lies at the core of this process, poses this question: "Do you have a safe person or persons in your life with whom you can process your frustrations?"

Questions to Ponder

1. Think of the last time you felt personally encouraged by someone in your church. What did they do that made you feel that way?
2. How did my brief discussion on Hebrews 13:17 make you feel? Uncomfortable? Neutral? Encouraged that someone finally said it? Why might that passage be difficult to preach in your church?

PART III

WHATCHA GONNA DO WHEN THE BAD BOYS COME FOR YOU?

CHAPTER 7

OPEN UP WITH VULNERABILITY (DO YOU HAVE A SAFE CONFIDANT?)

On stage, I make love to 25,000 people, and then I go home alone.

—Janis Joplin

As I write this chapter, I'm sitting in a Panera restaurant down the street from the dentist who numbed me up two hours ago. I especially enjoy this place because the baker often comes around to offer patrons a free half scone. Today I've already eaten a lemon, a cinnamon, and a blueberry one. I feel a bit self-conscious, so I crumpled the containers they came in and hid them under my napkin. I don't want him to think I'm here just for the free stuff (even though I am). If he doesn't see the incriminating evidence, maybe he'll offer me another.

When I arrived, I overheard several older men chatting in a foreign language as they put sugar and cream in their coffees. Since I'm in my mid-fifties, "old" means anybody over seventy. (I am not old.) As I wrote, I noticed these guys had crowded around a table to enjoy each other's company. I carefully watched them interact, and I tried not to stare.

As they sipped their java, it was obvious they were friends, probably deep friends. I felt a tinge of sadness. As I mulled over why those emotions came, I didn't like my answer. I felt sad because sometimes I'm not sure I have enough truly close friends to fill a table. And I am not alone in that self-assessment.

One of today's most refreshing mega-church pastors, Craig Groeschel, wrote honestly about his loneliness, describing an experience when he preached to a thousand teens at a Christian camp. On the last night, several dozen came to Christ while several hundred others kneeled in humble repentance.

> *After the service was over, I retreated to my room—alone. God had just used me powerfully to help many people, and minutes later, I felt abandoned and desperate. Dozens of people stood, sat, milled, and slept not a hundred feet from my hotel door, yet they seemed a million miles away. I was hurting and alone, and I didn't understand why.*
>
> *A flood of tears took me by surprise. Then came the questions: I'm supposed to be there for everyone else. But what happens when I hurt? When I'm afraid? Or need acceptance? Or feel alone? Who ministers to the minister? One moment I was in front of a crowd, full of confidence. The next moment I was crying in the corner of a hotel room, honestly believing that no one cared whether I lived or died.*[1]

Every pastor has probably felt the same way at some point. The prophet Elijah did when he bolted from Queen Jezebel after a great spiritual victory. He then commiserated in a cave that he was maybe the only one left who followed God.[2] Ministry, in contrast to other vocations, often makes it difficult to process our pain.

Dr. Mark McMinn, former professor at Wheaton College, has extensively studied pastors, and writes, "A pastor having a difficult day may be expected to pray about it, whereas a surgeon may have a drink or two with his co-workers."[3] He also notes, "It is striking to see how rarely clergy turn to relationships outside their families for support."[4]

King Solomon, whom Scripture calls the wisest man who ever lived, understood our need for close friends.

As iron sharpens iron, so one man sharpens another.[5]

I observed yet another example of something meaningless under the sun: This is the case of a man who is all alone, without a child or a brother. . . .

Two people are better off than one, for they can help each other succeed. If one person falls, the other can reach out and help. But someone who falls alone is in real trouble. Likewise, two people lying close together can keep each other warm. But how can one be warm alone? A person standing alone can be attacked and defeated, but two can stand back-to-back and conquer. Three are even better, for a triple-braided cord is not easily broken.[6]

He also advised, "The more wise counsel you follow, the better your chances."[7] And the apostle Paul, who understood the value of close friends, speaks with deep gratitude for Epaphroditus, Timothy, Tychicus, Aristarchus, Mark, and Luke.[8]

So if the Scriptures value safe people and friendships, what does the research tell us? How are we doing? Unfortunately, not so well.

I interviewed Dr. Michael Ross, executive director of The Pastors Institute, who has worked with several thousand pastors in various capacities. He told me that the number one problem pastors face is isolation. In an inventory he developed that evaluates five areas in ministry, 1,086 pastors from 42 denominations revealed the difficulty most pastors encounter in discussing their own needs and weaknesses with others.

Gary Kinnaman (former mega-church pastor) and Alfred Ells

(founder-director of Leaders that Last) write, "Most people in full-time ministry do not have close personal friendships and consequently are alarmingly lonely and dangerously vulnerable."[9] Steve Arterburn has observed, "The men in the church who are least likely to have friend connections are pastors."[10] Focus on the Family discovered that nearly 42 percent do not have any accountability partner with whom they meet.[11] And the Alban Institute, an ecumenical organization that serves thousands of congregations through research and publishing, has learned that pastors tend to seek help from others only when they are in crisis "rather than allowing these resources to sustain and nourish them consistently."[12] In other words, we don't seek out safe people to help us process ongoing issues until they escalate into major crises. Even then, many still suffer alone.

The Barna Research Group discovered that only *10 percent* of pastors seek counsel from others to help manage church frustration. When these issues arise, nine out of ten face them alone or pass the issue on to somebody else to solve. Unfortunately, I've been in that 90th percentile group too often, and I've suffered for it.

David Kinnaman noted,

> *I was also a bit surprised to find how few pastors talk about interpersonal frustrations or personality dilemmas—as friends and compatriots might experience. However, upon reflection, this insight seems to have traction. Ancillary research we have conducted suggests that pastors struggle to have meaningful relationships and friendships within the church. Pastors are surprisingly lonely—and not always fully in touch with the causes of or solutions for the isolation.*

A 2006 Barna Research Group study discovered that 61 percent of pastors have few close friends.[13]

The process outlined in this and the next three chapters to help us deal with our frustration requires that we invite safe people into our lives; highlighted (in the center) below, this is the key to lasting change. Without safe people, we can seldom defeat ministry killers.

Going It Alone

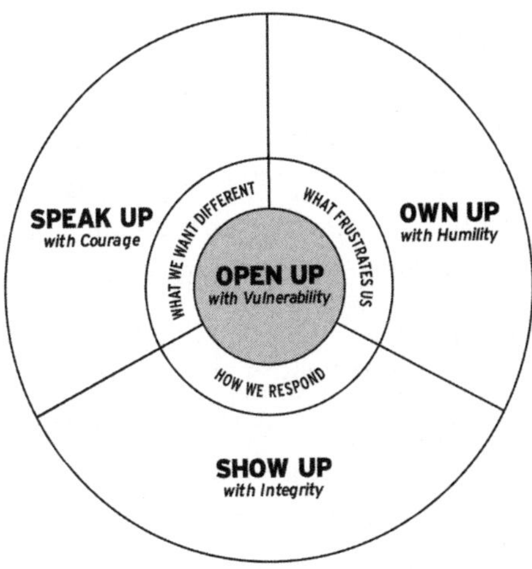

Some time ago a painful issue about my leadership in a previous church almost led me to throw in the towel. Seething anger and deep sadness about this situation had often left me on the verge of tears.

I faced a strong critic who wanted me out. I hadn't done anything immoral or unethical. I hadn't strayed from sound theology. I had, however, poorly led some staff and had become overbearing with them.

This person met with the elders, wrote a long letter listing my failures, and stirred up others in our church. When the matter escalated, the elders scheduled an overnight retreat to discuss the problems. I felt like I'd been called to the principal's office for an overnight lock-in. We had even consulted a lawyer who specialized in church conflict to facilitate our discussions. Fortunately, they eventually realized this issue didn't warrant my termination, and we experienced fruitful ministry in that church for several more years. And it turned out that I did need to make some changes in the way I led.

At that time, however, to my detriment, I faced it alone. I let my wife into some of my pain, but it would have been unfair to ask her to bear the brunt of all my hurt. So I bore much of it in private, and unresolved pain hindered God's work through me.

Shortly after the retreat, I attended a Bible conference at The Cove, a conference center in North Carolina run by the Billy Graham Association. On the drive there, I wept, railed at God, and vented my anger. After I arrived, I checked in and went to dinner. There the host introduced the speaker and the conference chaplain, who was available to pray with anyone who needed prayer. I certainly did.

After the first session, I went back to my room and shut my door, and an emotional vice-grip seemed to crush my heart. I wanted release and desperately wanted to talk to the chaplain, but I never mustered the courage. God had given me a safe opportunity to process my pain, but I took the lone-ranger approach and paid for it.

Although I prayed, journaled, and read Scripture during that painful time, I didn't invite a safe person into my life to help me navigate it. It took me two years to overcome the emotional bruises I received. I'm now convinced that had I invited a safe person in, I could have processed the frustration and pain much quicker and experienced more joy in ministry during the years that followed.

Why didn't I approach the chaplain? Why didn't I include someone back home to help? Why didn't I have a safe person in my life? Why do pastors go it alone so often?

When we discover what hinders close relationships, we're better able to overcome those obstacles and take steps to find safe people. After much reflection and much feedback from others through the years, I've discovered several factors that have contributed to my tendency to exclude safe people. I hope as you read about my struggles for intimate connection, you'll consider what might likewise hinder you.

I grew up in a middle-class Christian home, and although we weren't wealthy, my dad provided well for our needs. My parents loved me, believed in me, and still do. I wasn't a rebel. I had friends. I was a Boy Scout (even made Eagle). I did fine in school, but wasn't an athlete, though I tried out for basketball one year wearing sandals, and socks the color of cheddar cheese (I didn't make the team).

I was a geek, and geeks tend to communicate at a cerebral level. Unfortunately, as I grew up I didn't learn to communicate from my heart. I never talked much with my parents about feelings. The churches I attended seldom taught about healthy community or how to build close relationships. And I seldom talked to my friends at a deep level. I can't blame them or my parents for this struggle, but I know the lack of models for intimate communication diminished my ability to welcome safe people into my life. So one factor that has hindered me comes from childhood experience.

Another influence is my loner tendency. I once prided myself as mysterious, hard to get to know, Spock-like. In one way, this emotional distance served me well. It's a subtle technique we can sometimes use to control people; their not knowing what we're thinking or feeling keeps them on their toes and even a bit fearful of us. However, while this may work for a time, it eventually backfires. Those we need most, personally and professionally, will tend to shy away from us and mirror back what we mirror to them: distance. So my personality also made it difficult to find safe people.

My type-A inclination also has played a factor. I'm a high achiever, setting and reaching most of my goals and thus expecting a lot from myself and from others. Because my personal, and ministry, decisions are usually correct, I can be driven to be "right" to avoid being wrong and therefore looking weak. So I tend to conceal my struggles. As a result, people may view me as having my life all together with few problems. They may in turn feel they don't measure up around me, and then distance themselves from me.

In my heart, though, I know my struggles: sometimes disingenuous, sometimes saying what others want me to say, sometimes carefully weighing my words so I don't ruffle feathers or look dumb (or appear to be hurting). I don't like those tendencies. But God knows me and has tempered my weakness with painful ministry and family experiences, including what I've mentioned previously (one rebellious teen, and another with a brain tumor). He also gave me a wonderful, safe wife who's helped me learn to open up.

Another factor has affected me and probably many other pastors as well: *wounds*. Wounds come with the territory. To serve Christ means we serve hurting people. And hurt people hurt other people. Unprocessed wounds often lead us to guarded living. We begin to withdraw from others, at least by withdrawing our hearts. We crave intimacy yet fear it at the same time. Therefore, we put up walls, and in so doing can torpedo opportunities for close friendships. Just recently I had to fight my tendency to erect a wall after I experienced back-to-back wounds from a friend.

Facing Relational Anorexia

These four factors have worked against my building of close friendships: (1) a lack of formative modeling; (2) a loner tendency; (3) a personality type that can unintentionally push people away; and (4) wounds that can compel me to put up walls. One final factor I must add is also common to many pastors: Often we think that if people knew how we struggled, hurt, or had problems, it might lessen the respect they have for us and obstruct our effectiveness. Certainly we shouldn't publicly display all our dirty laundry, or we *would* diminish our influence. But actually, I've found that when I appropriately share my struggles, I endear myself to most people and they respect me more.

I'll never forget a story I heard Bill Hybels share at a conference. The specific details are hazy, but the impact it had on me remains. On one of his study breaks, he made a Sunday night visit to a small church. After the sermon, the pastor stood before his flock in tears and shared a heartbreak he had experienced with his son. He said he felt like a failure and wasn't sure what to do. He then closed the service. Spontaneously, the people rushed to the front and surrounded him, hugged him, and wept with him. Bill then used a term to describe the scene: "the circle of brokenness." As he drew thousands of us into this story, with misty eyes I yearned to feel that same acceptance in my church. I believe every pastor does.

If fear of rejection, looking less like a pastor, or worry that you might diminish your influence keeps you from inviting safe people in, realize the danger in which we can put ourselves. Without safe people, potential ministry killers can overwhelm us. A psychologist friend explained that this type of isolation often sets up pastors on a slippery slope toward sexual compromise. In our isolation, Satan will exploit our vulnerability. We can then begin to live secret sexual lives that may ultimately lead to ministry and/or marriage failure. Remember, sin grows easiest in darkness.

Unfortunately, church people can place us on a pedestal with unrealistic standards, expecting us to be perfect. Perhaps you've been burned when you shared a weakness or a failure with someone in your church. Such a rejection can lead us to fear that more rejections will follow if we continue to share our hearts with others. Thus, we breed further isolation.

We've probably all preached that God created us for deep relationship with others. But just as anorexia (the word actually means "no appetite") can cause a person literally to feel no hunger even though he is starving, relational anorexia can keep us from feeling our inner hunger for deep relationships. Henry Cloud and John Townsend's *Safe People* lists these indicators that we might have relational anorexia.

- *I am uncomfortable with people and relaxed when alone.*
- *I don't get "lonely," whatever people mean by that.*
- *I spend time with people out of obligation, or for functional reasons (tennis partner, commuting to work, etc.).*
- *My fantasies of vacation always involve my doing something fun by myself.*[14]

The authors also posed several questions that may indicate major hindrances to healthy relationships. I've paraphrased them here.

- *Do you tend to only be a giver in most of your relationships?*
- *Do others usually approach you only when they want something from you rather than to simply spend time with you?*
- *Do you find it difficult to open up to others?*
- *Do you most often choose to be alone to deal with your problems?*
- *Do you feel that only God really knows and loves you?*
- *Are intimate, two-way conversations with others rare?*[15]

Pastor, if any of these resonate with you, heed the message behind the famous Socratic words: "The unexamined life is not worth living." Find out what hinders you from developing close relationships. With the Holy Spirit's help, begin to move toward those who can come into your life to give you a safe place. If we can't truly connect with others, we may ultimately pick friends who won't connect with us. And those aren't the friends we want.

Lasting change requires that we allow others into our lives. We need safe people who will help us see our blind spots, encourage us to grow, and help us respond to ministry challenges in healthy ways. Research tells us that we actually need friendships to live long lives. Daniel Goleman, most known for his book *Emotional Intelligence*,[16] also co-wrote *Primal Leadership*, which says:

> *Three or more incidents of intense stress within a year (say, serious financial trouble, being fired, or a divorce) triple the death rate in socially isolated middle-aged men; they have no impact whatsoever on the death rate of men who cultivate many close relationships.*[17]

If we pastors are to experience longevity in ministry, we need safe people in our lives.

Goleman believes the greatest leaders excel in these four areas: self-awareness, self-management, social awareness, and relationship management. He writes that lasting change in leaders (and in our case, pastors) occurs through five key discoveries. One of these is opening ourselves up to safe people. He describes this as "developing supportive and trusting relationships that make change possible."[18] His insight tells us that to lead most effectively and to process our frustrations in healthy ways (and in our case, defeat ministry killers), we must seek out and develop safe relationships.

Profile of a Friend

So if safe people are crucial to our success and personal fulfillment, what do they look like, and how do we develop relationships with them?

For starters, a safe person is not perfect. I've never been drawn to those who seem to have no personal struggles, just like others weren't drawn to me when I appeared to have it all together.

December often reminds my wife and me that these "together" people don't really attract us. Every Christmas we receive several family newsletters, describing everyone's collective activities for the year. We enjoy most of these, but a few have consistently effused such glowing blessings, phenomenal children, and successful ministries that Sherryl and I don't even want to open them. (When our lives aren't going well, "perfect" people don't seem safe to us.)

We've discovered that *truly safe people carry their own wounds and scars, yet they don't allow themselves to get stuck in their pain. Rather, difficulties strengthen their character and make them appealing.*

Recently, during a sermon series on parenthood, I interviewed some psychologists on stage. One candidly shared about her failed marriages before she found Christ; she was now in a blended family and deftly fielded questions about her experience. As she answered, she portrayed a stage presence that reminded me of an old brokerage commercial, aired in the '80s and now posted on YouTube.

The ad goes like this: A kindergarten teacher asks her class who would like to recite the alphabet. One freckle-faced girl with short pigtails stands and begins to recite: "A, B, C, D, E, F . . . E F . . . E F Hutton!" Immediately the other students jump to their feet and lean toward her, paying close attention. As the camera pans back, the teacher also leans in, and a voice in the background states, "When E. F. Hutton talks, people listen."

When the psychologist spoke that morning, people listened. The lessons from her brokenness made her life attractive and enticing. Wounded and broken people who have grown through their failures often make some of the best safe people. They don't need degrees, pedigrees, or social status to qualify. Their softened spirits, tempered by life's hurts, overshadow even the most impressive résumés.

What *specific* qualities should we look for? Is it worth the risk to seek them out? Opening up to others does involve risk, and there's no guarantee those people will help us, but I'm convinced the potential benefits far outweigh the risks.

Before creating a checklist, perhaps my experience with a safe person can illustrate what to look for.

When I served in California as a teaching pastor, our church held an arts night that included music, drama, displayed paintings, and dessert. We'd crammed the paintings into the same room with a half dozen tables filled with cheesecake and drinks. I can't turn down cherry cheesecake, so during intermission I slipped in to get a piece. As I balanced my slice on a Styrofoam plate in one hand and my soft drink in the other, I feigned interest in the paintings on the easels (I'm *not* an art connoisseur). As I stood in front of one, I noticed out of the corner of my eye a guy about my age that I hadn't seen in church. I introduced myself, and immediately I felt drawn to him. That initial meeting left such an impression that I still remember it, though it occurred over ten years ago. His name was Mike.

Why was I drawn to him? He wasn't particularly striking. His clothes didn't impress me. He looked like an ordinary guy. His vocabulary didn't indicate superior education, although I learned later that he's quite intelligent. But when I spoke, he gave me his full presence. Even as I write this and reflect, something satisfying wells up inside me. When I met Mike that night, I felt that he really cared about what I had to say. His eyes said it. His smile said it. His body language said it. His spirit said it. I felt like he was there for me and me alone in those few moments. We didn't talk about anything deep, just small talk. And I didn't feel he expected me to be in "pastor mode."

Over the next three years we often met at the Taco Bell nearby. Every time, I felt that he was fully present for me. Even before Sunday services would start, when I'd chat with as many people as possible, Mike seemed to be there for me, even for a sixty-second conversation. I've met few people like him in my life. I've met lots of church people who come across guarded, disingenuous, or persistent in talking about themselves. Not Mike. He became a consistent safe person for me.

An important quality in a safe person is what I experienced with Mike: He will make himself fully present for you and show genuine interest in your life. To be sure, our relationship went both ways. In our conversations over those years, I also became safe for him. A healthy safe person not only will be fully present for you but also will welcome your presence into his life as each of you offer safety for the other.

As you consider the traits you'd look for in a safe person, consider these Scriptures and the guidelines they infer, because these people are often difficult to recognize.

When Samuel went to look for Saul's replacement, God told him,

> *Looks aren't everything. Don't be impressed with his looks and stature. I've already eliminated him. God judges persons differently than humans do. Men and women look at the face; God looks into the heart.*[19]

Outward impressions may belie the heart of a potential safe person, so don't let a poor first impression turn you off.

When David looked for those with whom he'd surround himself, he wrote,

> *I have my eye on salt-of-the-earth people—*
> *they're the ones I want working with me;*
> *Men and women on the straight and narrow—*
> *these are the ones I want at my side.*[20]

Character and integrity took front and center when he chose his advisors and leaders.

He also said,

> *Let the godly strike me!*
> *It will be a kindness!*
> *If they reprove me, it is soothing medicine.*
> *Don't let me refuse it.*[21]

David looked for those with the courage to tell him what he needed to hear, not what he wanted to hear. Goleman wisely notes,

> *People deprive their co-workers—whether bosses or subordinates—of honest performance feedback for several reasons, chief of which is that it can be uncomfortable to give such feedback. We're afraid of hurting others' feelings or otherwise upsetting them. Yet while we tend to keep the truth about how others are actually doing to ourselves (oddly, not just the negatives but also the positives), all of us generally crave that kind of appraisal. Candid evaluations matter deeply, in a way that other information does not.*[22]

When Paul taught about rights and privileges, he said, "Knowledge makes us proud of ourselves, while love makes us helpful to others."[23] Someone with all the right replies may not be who you need. Actually, we need those who will ask us the right questions more than those who want to give us answers.

Below I've listed several qualities to look for in a safe person. Only perfection, however, will embody them all, so don't expect to find someone who meets all the criteria. A safe person, however, should evidence many of these:

- *Not a cliché giver; doesn't over-spiritualize*
- *Asks good questions; effectively reflects back what he hears you say, and seeks to understand*
- *Believes in you*
- *Consistent; a promise keeper*
- *Trustworthy, can keep secrets*
- *Not afraid of your anger, tears, or other emotions*
- *Has his own scars yet doesn't wallow in his pain; empathetic*
- *Around him you don't feel like a child with a parent, but feel you are equals*
- *Will genuinely pray for and with you*
- *Not critical or judgmental*
- *Approachable, vulnerable, humble*
- *Wise and discerning*
- *Can and will challenge you to get outside your comfort zone*
- *Around him you feel comfortable; he'll let you be on the outside who you are on the inside*
- *Won't try to make you someone you're not; appreciates the real you*
- *Likeable to be around* (I can't overemphasize this)

- *Strong commitment to Christ; helps your commitment to Christ deepen*
- *Willing to confront with love and grace, doesn't flatter*
- *Helps you become a better person*
- *Doesn't have a lot of expectations of you*

To boil it down, a safe person is one who truly listens, occasionally offers advice, and consistently supports and strengthens you.

A Few Further Ideas

So where do we find a safe person? Is he or she in your church? Possibly. I have a safe person in my current church, an excellent leader who meets many of the criteria I listed above. He happens to be in the inner circle of our leadership, but I'm not responsible to him as I would be to the elders. You might find your safe person in your leadership group. However, be aware of an inherent tension. If you report to an elder or deacon board, a person on those boards may find it difficult to separate his church leadership role from the safe person role he could play in your life.

I experienced this with a safe person in my life; he later came onto our elder board. Before he made that decision, we discussed how our relationship might change. We agreed to be open-minded; if a tension between the two roles surfaced, his role as an elder would take priority over his safe-person role. Although we still meet and I consider him a safe person, his dual role as my "boss" and as my equal (as a safe person) has somewhat changed the dynamics.

One place you might look is in your local pastors' gatherings. Such a group offers an excellent "fishing pool," especially given the common experiences pastors share.

I once heard Gordon McDonald, a pastor for several decades, talk about how to find safe people. He suggested that we first list several potentially safe people within our current relationships. He then advised we take each one out to breakfast or lunch. From that group a few will surface with whom we would like to continue meeting. Over time, we will discover which of those with whom we best connect, with whom we have good chemistry, and with whom we could see ourselves spending more time.

Finding safe people takes work, discernment, and prayer. James encourages us to pray when he says, "You do not have, because you do not ask God."[24] And Scripture often portrays God inviting us to ask Him for help when we have a need: "If you need wisdom [if you want to know what God wants you to do], ask our generous God, and he will give it to you. He will not rebuke you for asking."[25]

One final caution: If you are a man, keep those safe relationships limited to other men. Likewise, if you are a woman, it's best to limit safe people to other women. You want to avoid intimate emotional relationships with others of the opposite sex.

Ultimately, at some point, we must step out in faith and ask that "someone" to be our safe person. One friend, who has been safe for me for over two decades, shared his thoughts with me. (If you give this book to your leaders, please mark this section to make sure they read it.)

> *In 1987, my wife and I moved to the Atlanta area, where I met Charles, a young pastor starting his first church. In those early days we met in a dance studio in a local strip mall. We joined that tiny church, and over the next two decades it grew to become a large and vibrant congregation in that community.*
>
> *In the course of my own Christian walk, and for more than twenty years, I have been blessed to serve Christ and the church as a teacher, deacon, elder, and in many other lay leadership roles. Interestingly, the most impactful role wasn't one with a traditional church title. It wasn't until a close friend of mine, an attorney, put a title to it that I understood it most completely. He called me a "pastor's encourager." Since then, I've realized how important such a role is to a pastor.*
>
> *During those years I discovered several important traits in this role*

that added energy and vitality to my pastor and friend that in turn infused life into the ministry of the church.

The foundational trait is time. You have to invest in the relationship, share life experiences, and spend time together to qualify. Often it's the simple things—one long late-evening meeting that ended up in a Steak-N-Shake with burgers and fries at 2 a.m.—talking, being guys, acting silly, and just being together. Sometimes it's serious, like the day we gathered around his youngest daughter, Tiffany, when she was only a year old to anoint her with oil as she faced brain surgery. I simply spent time with Charles.

Pastors often struggle with depression. Whether or not medical conditions are present, the pressure of pastoring, especially during stressful times in the ministry, brings much frustration, disappointment, and insecurity to pastors. Times of growth, change, disagreement, or difficulty often occur in the church and in people's personal lives. When they do, I've seen members, staff, and even the community expect the pastor to provide them a safe place to dump without judgment, without loss, and without risk. Charles needed an outlet, where he could process his emotions, a relief valve of sorts to relieve the hurts, disappointments, and insecurities without reprisal. I grew to become that safe place for Charles.

One of the most destructive sins in the church is gossip. It can wreck pastors and even split or destroy a church. Perhaps the greatest crisis in our ministry happened when a respected but misguided member disagreed with the leadership direction of the church and began privately to spread mistruths and make false accusations about the pastor to influence the church toward "his way." Sadly, I and the other leaders around Charles were young and slow to respond to the divisive gossiper. This lapse hurt Charles and risked damaging the church. Thankfully, we learned the practical application of Matthew 18. Afterward, I was quick to apply the lesson I learned—to quickly defend and protect not only truth in the church but also the reputation of my pastor.

When the relationship is truly secure there are occasions where real encouragement comes in a most unlikely manner: confrontation. When done gently, respectfully, privately, and out of love, it is "good medicine." I'm sure Charles remembers one evening when I invited him to my home. The two of us sat for hours in a wooden swing on the hill in my wooded backyard. We quietly talked about a serious staff situation that Charles had handled poorly and emotionally. Correction done with the right motive, in the right way, and for the right reason added to Charles' wisdom and confidence. I believe Charles wanted and needed that loving accountability. By the way, it went both ways and strengthened our friendship.

We all want and need people around us upon whom we can depend. We need those willing to stand with us when others oppose us, to hang in there when times are tough, and to remain when others abandon us. Jesus yearned for that from the disciples. Pastors especially need it when the church faces critical junctures. Charles depended on me to be there in those difficult times, just as Moses depended on Aaron and Hur to be there for him when he became weary.

I have known Charles and his family for over twenty years. We are both more seasoned, and hopefully wiser now. Although we live in separate parts of the country, he and I have forged an indelible mark of respect and friendship that transcends distance. It is Charles' wish and mine that every pastor would find a safe encourager.

—Hal

Exodus 17 tells the story of Aaron and Hur, to which Hal referred. As Joshua led the battle in the valley below, Moses interceded from the hill as he overlooked it. His raised arms signified his intercession, yet they grew so tired he could not keep them up any longer. Without Aaron and Hur to hold them up when he grew weary, the battle would have been lost. Many times Hal was like one of those men to me.

Pastor, I hope you will seek out a "Hal" in your life.

Before moving to the next chapter, where we'll examine what frustrates each of us personally, consider a final motivating statement about safe people. Two experts on pastoral leadership, Paul D. Stanley and J. Robert Clinton, write:

> *In our studies of leaders, we can clearly conclude with few exceptions that those who experienced anointed ministry and finished well had a significant network of meaningful relationships that inspired, challenged, listened, pursued, developed and held one another accountable. Those who failed to reach full maturity and finish well did not have it, or cut all or part of it off at some point.*[26]

One leader I greatly admire (as you've probably gathered by now) wrote these words: "I need a few safe people with whom I can process feelings of frustration so that I don't become emotionally toxic."[27] If somebody like Bill Hybels needs safe people, then every pastor does.

I want to finish well. I believe you do too. We must not take our journeys alone.

Questions to Ponder

1. Think about some safe people in your past. What qualities attracted you to them? Who in your current circle of friends evidences those same qualities?
2. If you don't have a safe friend, what about your personality might be hindering such relationships?
3. If you don't have a safe friend, now might be the time to seek one out. What steps could you take as early as next week to begin to find such a friend?

CHAPTER 8

OWN UP WITH HUMILITY (DOES WHAT FRUSTRATES YOU JIBE WITH SCRIPTURE?)

Sin is building your life and meaning on anything, even a very good thing, more than on God.[1]

—Tim Keller

Currently, I'm involved in two unique experiences in which I never would have envisioned myself. I'm seeing a shrink, and I've enrolled in an improv class at a local comedy club (a la *Whose Line Is It, Anyway?*).

A few years ago a friend who speaks professionally told me over lunch how his involvement in an improv class improved his speaking. After that conversation, I'd often considered enrolling. Finally, a few months ago, I took the plunge. I've completed three rounds of classes and have had my most fun in years. As a bonus, I've enjoyed some great spiritual conversations with people far from God.

In fact, recently I got an e-mail from my teacher about a possible small part in a movie being made in Chicago. And I auditioned, as a minister who performs a funeral in the remake of *Nightmare on Elm Street* (I guess for one of Freddy Krueger's victims).

A few weeks after I wrote this chapter, I found out I didn't get the part. Even so, as I thought about this small role, something satisfying welled up in me. Not that I watch slasher movies; I never even saw the original *Nightmare*. But at my last appointment with my counselor, he touched on something that may relate to this sense of satisfaction.

I mentioned earlier that my daughter Heather and I co-wrote *Daughters Gone Wild—Dads Gone Crazy,* a book about her rebellious teen years. My wife and I often went with her to counseling, but the focus was on her, not us. As I began to write this book, I evaluated what significantly frustrated me about ministry and kept sensing that some broken places inside me amplified those frustrations. I want my life's next decade to be the most fruitful for Christ, yet I kept feeling *something* was holding me back. So I called around and found a counselor who's also a pastor. I chose him because I assumed he'd give solid perspective on my experiences.

At that last meeting I explained that when people compliment me about something I do in the church, I appreciate it yet don't feel very satisfied afterward. I then described how I feel when someone in my improv class compliments me. One guy who calls himself an atheist remarked one night how he liked my humor in one of my skits. I felt deeply satisfied, and that stuck with me.

The counselor remarked, "It sounds like that's the little boy in you wanting to come out." I know this sounds like shrink-eze, but his comment stirred something deep inside me. Throughout this process I'm learning to more fully own my feelings and thoughts, and this ownership idea threads itself into this chapter's focus.

I now want to examine the second part of the process I suggest to help us thrive as we respond to ministry killer–type issues that can grind us down. This phase is about *Owning Up with Humility.*

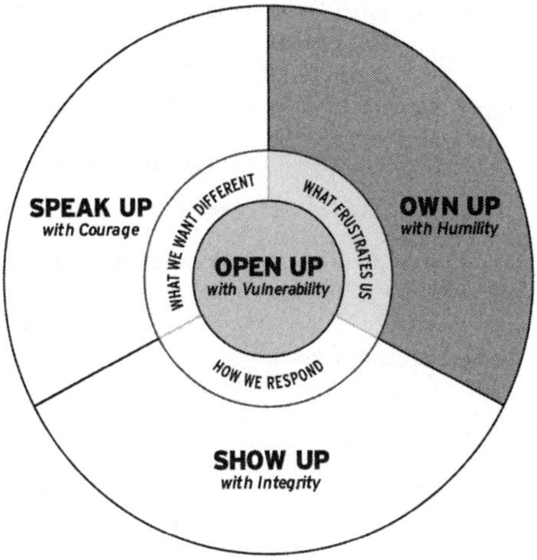

Chapter 7 asserted that for us to become most healthy and effective we must welcome safe people into our lives (*Open Up with Vulnerability*). With that core commitment in the center, this diagram displays the three other parts of the process.

- *Own Up with Humility* opens with the question "What really frustrates me?"
- *Show Up with Integrity* (see chapter 9) begins with the question "How do others see me handle my frustrations, and what should change?"
- *Speak Up with Courage* (see chapter 10) starts with the question "Who needs to know how I feel, and how should I communicate?"

In this chapter, I suggest we ask ourselves the following questions: The first, *What frustrates me most,* requires that we humbly own up to what bothers us about ministry, even if our frustrations seem unspiritual. The second leads us to compare those issues against Scripture: *Do my frustrations line up with appropriate biblical ones?* The third, *What frustrations need to change,* hopefully will challenge us to realign those issues with what truly should bother us—what matters most to God.

Awareness of Self and of Others

The day I worked on this chapter, I checked my Twitter page and discovered that the pastor of one of America's largest churches just began to tweet. Within two days he had 2,934 followers. I started two weeks prior and only had forty-four. I attended seminary about the same time he did; we're about the same age. I confess that unpleasant emotions have surfaced when I've read about his latest bestselling book or his latest Twitter feed about another mega-church pastor he just took to lunch. Is this jealousy, envy, insecurity, or a mixture of all three? I'm not sure. I'm truly glad God has used him so much, but as I compare my success, I sometimes feel very insignificant. I identify with these admissions from Jack Hayford, a well-known pastor and author in California.

> *I confess to sporadic bouts of doubt and cynicism. These intrusions of carnality into my pastor heart spring from the temptation to play the church numbers game, creating my pastoral self-image based on attendance figures. I thought when I finally led a large congregation I'd be able to shed the demeaning sense of inadequacy the game provokes in me. Not so. I still wrestle at times with a hideous smallness in my soul, just as I did years ago when Anna and I planted a church that zoomed from zero to forty-five in four years.*
>
> *I lived in the shadow of three-digit attendance figures. I thought the day I broke 100, a peace would fill my soul. When it happened, solace was temporary, and soon I was haunted again. Only the numbers had changed.*[2]

Bill Hull echoed similar thoughts.

> *At age fifty, I found myself successful but unsatisfied. I was hooked on results, addicted to recognition, and a product of my times. I was a get-it-done leader who was ready to lead people into the rarified air of religious competition. Like so many pastors, I was addicted to what others thought of me.*[3]

A counselor friend helped me understand how our hidden areas influence what we think, feel, and do. He drew a diagram that psychologists use to help people become more self-aware in their relationships. It's called the Johari Window.

Johari Window

	Known to self	Not known to self
Known to others	Arena	Blind Spot
Not known to others	Façade	Unknown

You can see that the blocks in the right column picture areas in our lives of which we're unaware. The blind spots are known by others but not by us; the unknown is hidden both to us and to others. The lower left hand block represents those areas we know about ourselves but others don't.

In this chapter, two of these blocks have bearing: the façade and the blind spot. If we honestly and appropriately disclose our struggles (façade), and if we humbly seek to become more self-aware (blind spots), we will lead and serve more effectively.

Unfortunately, we pastors don't do so well with self-awareness or with the awareness of others. For example, a 2006 Barna Group research report discovered that pastors believe 70 percent of adults in their churches "consider their personal faith in God to transcend all other priorities."[4] A contrasting survey revealed that only 23 percent of church people named faith in God as their top priority,[5] a large awareness miss for pastors.

Russ Veenker told me that lack of *self*-awareness tops the list of pastoral problems he has seen in the hundreds of pastors he's counseled. He said we should pay more attention to the truth in Romans 12:3: "Be honest in your estimate of yourselves."[6] He also noted that those who are more self-aware become much healthier pastors.[7]

Another survey on body care reinforces our apparent myopia. The vast majority of us describe our health as good, very good, or excellent, yet the data from the same body-mass index survey indicate that 78 percent of male pastors and 52 percent of female pastors are either overweight or obese.[8]

Finally, in an Ellison Research study, Ron Sellers noted the difference between how pastors see their own family health and the health of other clergy families.

> *Ministers apparently have a much more optimistic view of their own family than they do of the families of other ministers. When one out of every twenty ministers feels his or her own family unit is unhealthy, but one out of every seven ministers believes the family units of others in their denomination are unhealthy, there's a disconnect.*[9]

Because distortions and blind spots can warp self-awareness, it's even more important that we invite safe people into our lives. That's why the core of this four-part process is *Open Up with Vulnerability*. We need safe people to help us see our blind spots; the greater our leadership influence, the less likely we accurately assess ourselves in critical leadership areas.[10]

What Frustrates You Most?

I hope the first part of this chapter will encourage you to clearly name and specifically call out what gets under your skin. I've combined into the chart below the list of frustrations from the Barna Group and the LifeWay research. Take a few moments and check off the top seven to ten issues that immediately come to mind regarding what bothers you most or keeps you awake at night. Do this exercise on a Monday morning or after a board meeting for the most accurate results. Be totally honest, even if you feel weak, selfish, or unspiritual. If you have a safe friend or two, this might be a good time to seek their input on what they perceive frustrates you.

Top Frustrations Caused by Church People

___ *Lack of commitment and follow-through*

___ *Lack of commitment to serve in ministry*

___ *Lack of faithfulness, inconsistent Christian living*

___ *Communication, misunderstandings among the people*

___ *Lack of involvement, reluctance to participate*

___ *Resistance to change, narrow-mindedness*

___ *Absenteeism, sporadic attendance*

___ *Financial issues, budget, stewardship*

___ *Lack of time, busyness, schedule-overloading by the people*

___ *Expectations of me: unclear, unrealistic, conflicting, unmet*

___ *Apathy, indifference, lukewarm attitudes*

___ *Pettiness, bickering, complaining, criticizing, minor disagreements*

___ *Marriage disharmony, infidelity, divorce*

___ *Immaturity*

___ *Spiritual disobedience, unwillingness to repent of sin*

___ *Lack of vision/ministry-direction consensus issues*

___ *Gossip, slander, betrayed confidences*

___ *Interpersonal relationship problems*

___ *Church not a priority; secular activities trump church*

___ *Hesitancy with evangelism/witnessing, lack of outreach*

___ *Control issues, territorial battles*

___ *Poor conflict resolution*

___ *Pastor's limitations; can't be/do everything for everyone*

___ *Family conflict, poor parenting*

___ *Lack of respect for others: discourteousness, unkindness, lack of love, lack of empathy*

___ *Alcohol and drug problems*

___ *Lack of spiritual growth*

___ *Generational challenge, relevance*

___ *Lack of community involvement, social inaction*

___ *Selfishness, consumerism*

___ *Worship style, music*

___ *Falling away, backsliding, leaving the church*

___ *Discouragement, depression, despair, negativity*

___ *Lack of respect for authority and leadership*

___ *Lay leadership issues: disunity, ineffectiveness, passivity*

Other: ________________________________

Other: ________________________________

Other: ________________________________

Other: ________________________________

Remember, these are behaviors and attitudes you see in the people in your church. If other things frustrate you, write them beside "Other." Now write those issues in one of the categories in the boxes below: church and/or leadership issues, spiritual-growth issues, or relationship issues. I've put my issues in the first chart as an example.

Church/leadership issues	**Spiritual-growth issues**	**Relationship issues**
1. financial issues 2. unclear expectations 3. unrealistic expectations 4. lack vision consensus 5. church not a priority 6. little affirmation from significant people	1. consumerism 2. inconsistent Christian living	1. pettiness 2. no empathy

Church/leadership issues	Spiritual-growth issues	Relationship issues
________________	________________	________________
________________	________________	________________
________________	________________	________________
________________	________________	________________
________________	________________	________________

We *must* humbly acknowledge our issues. The more self-aware we become, the more we can take constructive action in areas detrimental to us, our families, and our churches. Through my process, I'm also learning why these things bother me so much.

One humorous yet sad response I received from a frustrated pastor involved a conversation he'd had. One of his deacons was sharing about a recent dream in which he saw someone else (not the pastor) preaching. This was an indirect way of telling the pastor he wanted him gone. This pastor said he later learned this deacon wanted one of his friends to be pastor instead. Neither you nor I would want to hear that from a leader.

Do Your Frustrations Square With Scripture?

I remember the first Bible I got as a child. My mom and dad took me to church regularly. I even joined and was dunked when I was about seven, although I didn't have a real relationship with Christ. It took me a few years to understand what that involved.

When I finally committed my life to Jesus, I was baptized and joined a local church under the right auspices. However, after the first "joining," that church gave me a Bible. *Holy Bible* was emblazoned in gold print across the front of the heavy black cardboard cover.

It was inexpensive, and after a few months the tissue-thin pages began to fall out. The coolest part of that Bible, however, was that it was an official KJV Red-Letter Edition. Since the red print stood out, I'd often read only those words. I finally figured out that everything in red was spoken by Jesus.

It'd been years since I'd read a Bible with Jesus' words in red, but I tried it recently and found it enlightening. That's the exercise I'd like you to try now: Grab a red-letter edition and read only Jesus' words. If you can't find a hard copy, there are several online.

As you read, ask yourself this question: "What concerns Jesus most?" A quick reading of His words in Matthew alone reveals that these issues bothered Him: missing the kingdom, misplaced priorities, lack of love, hypocrisy, lack of faith, judgmental attitudes, pride, broken relationships, lack of forgiveness, and no regard for the poor and needy. If all the words of Paul or David or Moses were in green, we'd see similar themes. Jesus says little or nothing about strategic planning, smooth-running organizations, or goal setting. His major concerns dealt with matters of the heart.

Once more: We *can't* ignore leadership and organizational issues. We must wisely steward our resources. These issues do take time, and they do require our attention. And they will frustrate us. But we must put those matters in their proper place.

Perhaps an experience in Jesus' life best illustrates how organizational issues often compete with heart issues for our attention.

Mary and Martha, the two sisters of Lazarus, had invited Jesus over for dinner one day. Luke records this story, which I find both convicting (because I'm too much like Martha) and encouraging (because I aspire to be more like Mary).

> *As Jesus and his disciples were on their way, he came to a village where a woman named Martha opened her home to him. She had a sister called Mary, who sat at the Lord's feet listening to what he said. But Martha was distracted by all the preparations that had to be made. She came to him and asked, "Lord, don't you care that my sister has left me to do the work by myself? Tell her to help me!"*
>
> *"Martha, Martha," the Lord answered, "you are worried and upset about many things, but only one thing is needed. Mary has chosen what is better, and it will not be taken away from her."*[11]

Martha had allowed lesser issues to distract her from the most important one. Jesus, God himself, was in her living room and wanted her attention. He was most concerned about her heart, not a chicken casserole.

Her administrative project took precedence over people. She even vented her frustration at Jesus because He didn't notice Mary's apparent irresponsibility. I wonder how much Martha was motivated to make herself look competent and in control. In her case, the urgent trumped the important.

I don't mean to beat up on Martha or to elevate the contemplative life above the life of action. We pastors need Martha-like drive and a bias *toward* action. After all, we see Martha's exceptional abilities in the fact that she owned the house. But based on Jesus' comment about Mary, Martha seemed to have misordered her priorities.

Jesus said *one thing is needed.* Mary understood that He was the anchor for her soul. She didn't want to miss the opportunity to be in His presence. The Lord's response to busyness and attentiveness illustrates our need to prioritize spiritual and relational issues over organizational ones.

Unfortunately, when we begin to invest our energies into what matters most to God's heart, we won't necessarily see instant results and may even find this choice quite difficult. Most of the prophets saw little immediate results from their preaching. Jeremiah, aptly called the weeping prophet, grieved over the rebellious, stiff-necked people of Israel. Their disobedience often broke his heart.

> *Oh, that my head were a spring of water*
> *and my eyes a fountain of tears!*
> *I would weep day and night*
> *for the slain of my people.*[12]

Yet God promised to sustain him.

> *"They will fight against you but will not overcome you, for I am with you and will rescue you," declares the Lord.*[13]

Paul faced the challenge to right the early church's theological errors as well as address their relational problems. Even so, he wrote that he would "continue for [their] progress and joy in the faith."[14] He believed God's grace was sufficient to sustain him.[15]

Jesus himself was not immune to such disappointment. Although Satan could not conquer Him and the Pharisees could not sway Him, the people grieved Him:

> *O Jerusalem, Jerusalem, you who kill the prophets and stone those sent to you, how often I have longed to gather your children together, as a hen gathers her chicks under her wings, but you were not willing!*[16]

When we realign our focus to the important and with grace face the inevitable resistance, we please God's heart. David Goetz, former editor of *Leadership Journal*, nailed it with these words:

> *What we enjoy, after being released from the need for significance and success, is the sweetness of the obedience. Finding one's purpose comes not from the results of service but from the act of obedience. No matter what the call—resettling refugees, championing affordable housing for the poor or cheap drugs to combat AIDS, fighting for human rights, or the simple act of buying a cup of coffee for an older woman who sits alone on the bench outside Starbucks—inner liberty comes as I pursue truth, justice, and righteousness without needing to be seen as right or needing to see results.*[17]

Which Frustrations Need to Change?

In the list of Top Frustrations Caused by Church People you created a few pages prior, if most of yours fell in the last two categories, you've probably put your focus in the right place. If most of them fell in the first category, like me, you need to reexamine them and begin to elevate those nearest God's heart over the others.

So how do we do that? How do we begin to push organizational matters down the priority list? Although I have a long way to go, I've discovered a few helpful tips.

I don't sit on the platform during the music part of our services, as did the pastors of the churches where I grew up. As a kid I always wondered why some remained seated in the red-velvet-covered chairs on the platform when everybody else stood for worship. I've seen preachers who, while they sit, just stare at their Bibles in their laps. (Were they finishing up their sermon?) I've seen others grimace. (Was the music that bad?)

I stand during the music time and always sit stage left, second chair, first row. Until I get up to speak, I can't see how many people are in our auditorium. I don't want to be obvious by turning around, so I've tried to gauge attendance peripherally. If the place looks full, I get pumped; if I see lots of empty chairs, I feel a bit down.

Now, however, instead of focusing on attendance, I try to focus my thoughts and prayers on the people's hearts and on the Lord himself. I find that when I pray for those attending that morning to take a step closer to Jesus, low attendance doesn't bother me as much. My first suggestion is this: *Before you get up to speak, pray for the hearts of those who* are *there that day, and try not to focus on those who aren't.*

The second idea involves *unspoken self-talk,* which can profoundly influence our state of mind. Usually after each service I chat with people in the lobby. I would often silently ask myself, "Is this person going to say something good about my message?" and I expected affirming comments. If someone didn't say something positive, my self-talk would turn negative ("Charles, you must have blown it. I guess they didn't like the message. I knew it wasn't going to connect"). Then the expectation for affirmation would grow with each new conversation. I began to inwardly demand encouragement, and when I didn't get it I'd feel discouraged. As a result, those people touches became all about me and how they perceived me.

I'm now trying to *change my inner dialogue.* When I chat with others, I'm trying to listen from my heart to make myself truly present for them. I'm discovering a delightful result: inner peace and a greater sense of God's pleasure.

The third tip ties in to a church's weekly statistical reports. Mondays are seldom a pastor's favorite day. If you're like me, you're exhausted from Sunday's activities. My ministry "hangover" usually lasts until mid-Tuesday.

Usually by mid-afternoon Monday I'll get the attendance and giving report via e-mail. Previously, first thing Monday morning, I'd check with our financial department to get an advance report. A good report would make my day; a bad one would put a damper on everything. However, *I've stopped asking for an early report, and I now wait until it comes to me.* I'm intentionally refusing to let a bad report control my day. It's working. Because I'm focusing less on the numbers, my joy is not torpedoed when they aren't good.

One final lesson comes from David Kinnaman's comments on the Barna Group survey:

> *First, it strikes me that the frustrations and disappointments identified by pastors are much more in line with what an employer feels about his employees than what a parent might feel toward his children—or better yet, what a friend might feel toward fellow "co-laborers." I realize that there is a leadership dynamic in play within a church, but I wonder the degree to which pastors view congregants as not living up to the standards they expect. It's a subtle form of condescension that can creep in what otherwise would be a "holy discontent" (as Bill Hybels would label it) about the condition of people's lives and hearts.*
>
> *Finally, while we did not directly probe this sentiment, we found little evidence that pastors have an overriding perspective that God's grace fills the cracks of inadequate relationships—to paraphrase a theme common in Dietrich Bonhoeffer's* Life Together. *As Bonhoeffer puts it, we don't bear one another's burdens; we bear the burden of each other. Few pastors seem to have this "higher view" of the sacred nature of life together, of being sons and daughters in God's family.*

This contrast between an employer-employee relationship and a parent-child relationship struck me. I wonder how much of the frustration I experience with the organizational/church stuff rises out of this subtle yet unintended expectation I have of the people. I wonder how often I have projected this attitude on them to "produce" to make the organization—and therefore, me—look good.

Paul writes,

> *You are witnesses, and so is God, of how holy, righteous and blameless we were among you who believed. For you know that we dealt with each of you as a father deals with his own children, encouraging, comforting and urging you to live lives worthy of God, who calls you into his kingdom and glory.*[18]

Since I've become more aware that I struggle with this tendency, I'm now seeing others differently and am more able to reorder what frustrates me.

One area where I still struggle is what I perceive as unrealistic expectations of me by key leadership. My counselor has helped me see that this struggle may be rooted in my own childhood experiences. As you discover what you need to change, consider professional counseling as an option to help root out some of these deeper issues. Please don't feel you are less of a leader if you take that step. In fact, if you do, you are showing courage and humility, two strong character traits.

As you begin to shift what frustrates you, don't expect a Holy Grail, a silver bullet, or a panacea. Life this side of heaven will always be messy. If your ministry has etched frustrations into you, lasting change will take time. Old habits die hard. Yet as we surrender to the Lord and experience His grace, He will bring the changes we need. *The Message* paraphrase captures the challenge we face.

> *Sometimes we can hardly wait to move—and so we cry out in frustration. Compared to what's coming, living conditions around here seem like a stopover in an unfurnished shack, and we're tired of it!* [19]

In this chapter, we've examined the second phase, *Own Up with Humility*. You've uncovered your specific frustrations, determined how they line up biblically, and begun to reprioritize them. D. A. Carson speaks candidly on this subject when he comments on 1 Corinthians 3:13 ("Each one's work will become manifest, for the Day will disclose it, because it will be revealed by fire, and the fire will test what sort of work each one has done"):[20]

> *This ought to be extremely sobering to all who are engaged in vocational ministry. It is possible to "build the church" with such shoddy materials that at the last day you have nothing to show for your labor. People*

may come, feel "helped," join in corporate worship, serve on committees, teach Sunday school classes, bring their friends, enjoy "fellowship," raise funds, participate in counseling sessions and self-help groups, but still not really know the Lord.

If the church is being built with large portions of charm, personality, easy oratory, positive thinking, managerial skills, powerful and emotional experiences, and people smarts, but without the repeated, passionate, Spirit-anointed proclamation of "Jesus Christ and him crucified," we may be winning more adherents than converts. Not for a moment am I suggesting that, say, managerial skills are unnecessary, or that basic people skills are merely optional. But the fundamental nonnegotiable, without which the church is no longer the church, is the gospel, God's "folly," Jesus Christ and him crucified.[21]

As we focus on equipping people for better relationships and obedience to Christ, I believe the end result *will* positively impact organizational and church issues. And ministry killers will lose their power. In the next chapter, we'll delve into the third step, *Show Up with Integrity*, by examining how we currently respond to our frustrations.

Questions to Ponder

1. Do you agree with the quote from Tim Keller at the beginning of this chapter? Why or why not? Do you ever find that what drives you to do well in ministry can sometimes displace God?
2. What do you think others would tell you might fit into your "blind spot" box in the Johari Window?
3. Were you surprised at the list of frustrations you compiled? Should you begin to make any specific steps to reprioritize those issues? If so, what steps?

CHAPTER 9

SHOW UP WITH INTEGRITY (ARE MY RESPONSES TO MINISTRY FRUSTRATIONS HEALTHY?)

After twenty-five years of priesthood, I found myself praying poorly, living somewhat isolated from other people, and very much preoccupied with burning issues. Everyone was saying that I was doing really well, but something inside was telling me that my success was putting my own soul in danger.[1]

—Henri Nouwen

Thus far we've covered two steps in the process to help us deal with our frustrations and defeat ministry killers. First, *Open Up* with Vulnerability focused on finding safe people who can help us manage and understand our frustrations. Second, *Own Up* with Humility encouraged us to honestly admit what frustrates us. Third, *Show Up* with Integrity involves what we do in response to those issues. In this step I suggest we evaluate how we respond to frustrations so that we actually can make appropriate changes.

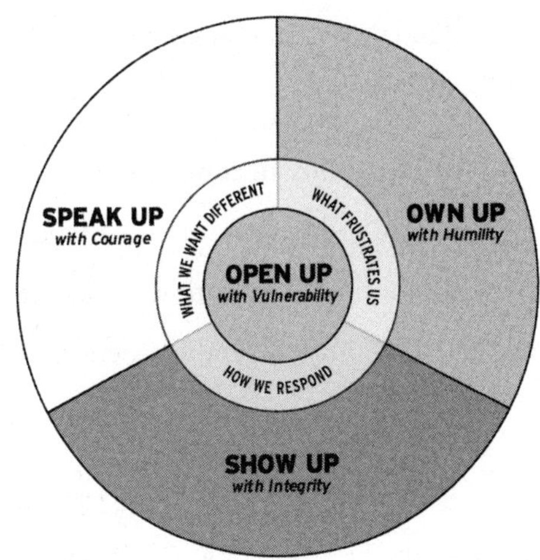

Recently my counselor asked me an awkward question: "Do you want to be worshiped?" My immediate response was, "Of course not. Worship is reserved for God himself." But he just stared back at me, and that was my cue to rethink my answer. As I pondered his question, then and in the days that followed, I believe he touched on a temptation with which ministry can entice.

We all would agree that we must only worship the God of the Bible. To worship something or someone is to ascribe to it the highest value possible, and what we worship reveals what's most important to us. Only God deserves that position.

However, aren't we tempted to relish the praise "adoring" church members give us? It feels wonderful to be the center of attention, to meet the pressing needs of hurting people, and to hear someone compliment us. Henri Nouwen described this temptation in saying, "It seems easier to be God than to love God, easier to control people than to love people, easier to own life than to love life."[2] I still wrestle with that question, because how I answer it impacts how I respond when things don't go my way. Our answer is tied to how I'm using the word *integrity.*

I'm not limiting integrity's meaning to the common definition: moral uprightness. I'm using a broader, more inclusive definition that Henry Cloud uses in his book *Integrity*:

> *When we are talking about integrity, we are talking about being a whole person, an integrated person, with all of our different parts working well and delivering the functions that they were designed to deliver. It is about wholeness and effectiveness as people.*[3]

Cloud notes throughout his book that integrity *integrates* these character aspects:

1. The ability to connect authentically
2. The ability to be oriented toward the truth
3. The ability to work in a way that gets results and finishes well
4. The ability to embrace, engage, and deal with the negative
5. The ability to be oriented toward growth
6. The ability to be transcendent

When we live lives of integrity as pastors (that is, we *Show Up* with Integrity), like a boat, the wake we leave in our path will make God, not us, the object of worship. Again, Jonathan Edwards' story (from the introduction) encourages me on several levels. First, even the most brilliant and godly will face potential ministry killers. Second, when we respond to church problems with integrity, we leave a powerful impression on others that can change their hearts. Third, when we respond appropriately to ministry difficulties, ultimately God is glorified.

So what do you do with frustrations and the temptation to yield to ministry killers? Earlier we examined the research that described how we pastors respond to them. I used animal metaphors to describe the most common responses. If you were to pick the one that best describes you, which would you choose? I've put in parentheses the percentages of pastors who indicated each one.[4]

- *The Turtle*: The Lord and I can work this out in prayer and through the Word. (51%)
- *The Lion*: I immediately face the issues head on. (34%)

- *The Skunk*: I'll let others handle these frustrations so I don't have to face them. (15%)
- *The Sloth*: I tend to be detached from frustrations because I don't believe I have any, or else none come to mind. (13%)
- *The Hawk*: It's somebody else's fault. (By implication, many of us are guilty of this because only 2% of us look to ourselves as the cause of the frustration.)

Take a moment and think about your last Sunday afternoon, or Monday morning, or the day after your last board meeting. What frustrated you most? What got under your skin? What did you keep rehearsing in your mind? How did you treat your family, your leaders, and those you don't particularly like? What was your body telling you? Did headaches, stomachaches, muscle pains, or lack of sleep become more prevalent?

Gary McIntosh and Samuel Rima describe our unhealthy responses as "dark sides," defining this as "our inner urges, compulsions, motivations, and dysfunctions that drive us toward success or undermine our accomplishments." This "develops slowly over a lifetime of experiences and is often revealed in moments of frustration or anger."[5] Leaders "who are aware of their dark side and are willing to deal openly and honestly with it before God are empowered for greater effectiveness."[6]

As you examine yourself, don't just lean on self-analysis. The apostle Paul didn't when facing a difficult issue in the Corinthian church. They were choosing sides about their favorite preacher, and after directly addressing this issue he wrote these words:

> *So look at Apollos and me as mere servants of Christ who have been put in charge of explaining God's mysteries. Now, a person who is put in charge as a manager must be faithful. As for me, it matters very little how I might be evaluated by you or by any human authority. I don't even trust my own judgment on this point. My conscience is clear, but that doesn't prove I'm right. It is the Lord himself who will examine me and decide.*[7]

Although he felt confident that his conscience was clear, Paul didn't trust it as the final arbiter: He recognized that the Lord would ultimately decide.

Recommendations for Responding

Here are a few suggestions that, when used together, can probably give us an accurate idea of how others perceive our responses.

Obviously, we must begin by inventorying ourselves, honestly examining both our internal and external worlds when church people frustrate us. If you've picked one of the animal descriptions that reflect the research, go deeper. Specifically, how do you relate to a leader or a church member who consistently gets under your skin? What do you say to yourself in your mind? What do you say to them? What do you really want to say? Physically, what sensations do you feel? What emotions surface?

Often our feelings give clues; we must listen to our emotions and ask ourselves why we feel as we do. If we don't, it's like trying to see with one eye. Centuries ago, St. Ignatius wrote that one means through which the Lord reveals himself is in the deepest movements of our feelings.[8]

First, I've found that keeping a *journal* helps me identify and process unpleasant emotions. I've learned that when I honestly record my thoughts and feelings about myself and about how I feel toward others, I discover patterns, both healthy and unhealthy. When I pinpoint those patterns, I'm then able to make course corrections; the initial step to solving any problem is to define it.

Second, we should involve our *safe friends*. They can help us see responses and reactions we otherwise would miss. One of my friends noticed that I sometimes became defensive in a group of leaders. He helped me see that when I talked one-on-one with him, I seldom became defensive, but not so in a board meeting if someone said something untrue that might make the others think less of me. With his help, I recognized that my defensiveness had become my unconscious way of attempting to control what they thought about me. He and the others felt my attempts to manipulate. I never would have seen this blind spot had he not risked sharing his observation.

Third, consider taking some *inventories* that can shed light on our personality and how others perceive us. The most well-known personality inventory, DISC, comes in many versions. Most include insights about how your personality tends to respond under pressure. One helpful online tool, the 360-degree assessment, seeks anonymous feedback in key areas from those you supervise, those who supervise you, and your peers. When I took the assessment, it hit me hard in revealing some weaknesses others saw in me. This enabled me to begin to change some of the ways I was "showing up" to others. Another tool you might find useful is the emotional intelligence assessment, which looks at self-awareness, self-management, social awareness, and relationship management, all factors that leadership experts agree are crucial for healthy leading.

Finally, to help balance how we assess our responses, I suggest this simple word picture, a triangle. Instead of basing your assessment on one perspective, combine these three. Healthy introspection and self-assessment have their place; again, though, don't rely on them alone. Invite safe people into the process, and seek God's perspective through prayer and Scripture. If we incorporate all three of these "legs," we'll get a clearer picture of how we respond to nagging church issues.

When I wrote the majority of this book, I faced an ongoing struggle in my church. Previously I noted that most of my frustrations have fallen in the organization/leadership category. As I unpack that key issue in the rest of this chapter, I hope the steps I took might encourage you to face your biggest frustration.

My strongest character traits include perseverance, discipline, and the ability to clearly think through a situation. As a result, I've prided myself on my ability to land on two feet when I face hardship. Because I have lone-ranger tendencies, initially I tend to disengage from people to process my pain. Thus, I usually don't visibly react in anger to others or strong-arm them to get my way. I tend to be more like the Turtle at first, introspective. I assume "God and I can work this thing out."

Unfortunately, I can then morph into the Lion and rashly confront. The particular issue with which I struggled involved our elders' desire to examine our leadership structure. In a few consecutive meetings I sensed their dissatisfaction with our current structure: with me as the lead visionary and primary directional leader. We then scheduled meetings to bring together our pastors, elders, and deacons (responsible for the facilities and finances) to brainstorm how a high-performing team should look.

During this time I prayed, consulted Scripture, and often journaled. I tried independently (with God's help) to resolve my inner angst. When I attended the meetings, I began to disengage from the conversation, which became obvious to the other leaders. My faulty thinking fooled me into believing that by withdrawing I would not unduly influence their final decision. In reality, I disengaged so I could protect myself from owning any part of a final decision that might not be the best for the church, or one that I preferred.

Although I physically pulled back, inside I waged a war. I would mentally argue my case with these other leaders and vicariously experience worst-case scenarios. I felt exhausted because nothing ever got resolved. I would confess my sin of worry, call my internal dialogue sin, quote Scripture, and pray constantly. But I was not at peace. This drama seemed to be on an endless repeating loop. I felt like the proverbial hamster running as fast as he can in a wheel, expending loads of energy yet getting nowhere.

About that time I began to see my counselor. He helped me understand that I can never resolve anything while disengaged. After a few sessions and a conversation with an older elder, I had an epiphany. The way I was responding to this frustration was with anything but integrity. I was self-serving, harming the team, and displeasing God. When I finally admitted to the elders that my faulty thinking had wrongly led me to disengage and that I would now begin to engage, I was surprised at their response. As I became vulnerable and willing to engage, what I desired from them—that they support and believe in me as their leader—happened. I also felt at peace for the first time in quite a while.

At that time I wasn't sure if the final leadership decision would go my way, but I believe that when I admitted my unhealthy response and changed, I honored God by *Showing Up* with Integrity. My healthy response not only brought me peace but helped me begin to connect more deeply to my leadership. A few weeks after I completed this chapter, the elders made their final decision and it was everything I could have wanted. But God already had changed my heart.

Perhaps my honesty and vulnerability bridged the silent gap (between our elders and me) that Julia Duin writes about in *Quitting Church:*

> *[The laity] wonder if their spiritual leaders have real lives. They have had it with pastors who have no clue what a typical workday is like or what it's like to commute, put up with day care, or deal with numerous other challenges that most of the congregation must face every day.*[9]

I became more real to these leaders when I admitted I'm a normal person who messes up sometimes. In doing so I believe I defeated a potential ministry killer.

This change would not have occurred had I not invited a safe person into my life (the core of the process, as you'll recall, is *Open Up* with

Vulnerability). In this case, I paid somebody, a counselor. I needed someone objective with whom I felt safe and who could help me understand how I was showing up. He helped me see how my showing up affected other leaders. You may not need a counselor, but I can't overstate that we all need those who will provide loving, objective feedback.

As we appropriately engage with those we serve and those who irritate us, we'll inevitably face this tension to stay healthy. Eugene Peterson, author of *The Message* paraphrase, describes this in his answer to a question about how to stay rightly engaged:

> *A term that occurs in the literature of the spiritual masters is detachment. Now, detachment is the cultivation of a relationship that is present but not taking ownership, not being messianic or managerial. It gives the other person freedom—it allows the "other" to be "other."*
>
> *This way of relating requires detachment from a "need-based" relationship. It is inherent in the gospel, but it's easy for it to get skewed by sin or co-opted by sin in the guise of compassion. I love the phrase in T. S. Eliot's* Four Quartets: *"Teach us to care and not to care."*
>
> *Caring, but not caring. They're both part of the same thing. It's an art. You make mistakes along the way. You don't learn it in your first year in the parish.*[10]

Do I still have this propensity to disengage and work things out privately with just God and me? Absolutely. Have I fully learned my lesson? Probably not. I'm still "bent" that way. But the more I respond to my issues in healthy ways, the more likely the next time I'm tempted to revert, I'll make the right choice. Daniel Goleman repeatedly states in *Primal Leadership* that we *can* make lasting changes in the crucial leadership areas, such as self-awareness, self-management, self-confidence, bond-building, and conflict management (the indicators a 360-degree assessment provides). So with God's help, we can truly change.

When I've honestly admitted my unhealthy responses, it hasn't been pleasant. No one wants to be found wanting, weak, or immature. But out of vulnerability come power and strength. Paul learned this after a mountaintop experience, when to keep him humble, God gave him what he called his tormenting "thorn in the flesh." After he repeatedly asked God to remove it and was refused, the Holy Spirit revealed the tremendous good and amazing power that were birthed as a result.

> *But he said to me, "My grace is sufficient for you, for my power is made perfect in weakness." Therefore I will boast all the more gladly about my weaknesses, so that Christ's power may rest on me. That is why, for Christ's sake, I delight in weaknesses, in insults, in hardships, in persecutions, in difficulties. For when I am weak, then I am strong.*[11]

As we pastors humbly admit our unhealthy responses, God will make us stronger servant-leaders.

Possibilities for Change

So how can we begin to change our unhealthy responses to healthy ones? Clearly once we realize what needs to change with God's help we must stop those behaviors and responses. But less direct choices may actually support lasting changes. I have a few ideas.

- *Do something totally different from ministry.* I've mentioned the improv class I joined, which gave me a refreshing break from ministry routine. Now I'm even thinking of taking a few acting classes just for the fun of it.
- *Be okay with taking care of you.* Pete Scazzero, who learned this the hard way, said: "The degree to which you love yourself corresponds to the degree to which you love others. Caring for ourselves was difficult for us to do without feeling guilty. We unwittingly thought that dying to ourselves for the sake of the gospel meant dying to marital intimacy and joy in life. We had died to something God had never intended we die to."[12]
- *Keep healthy boundaries with others.* A boundary is a line that helps

define those things for which we are responsible. They define who we are and who we are not; when properly managed they can bring us great freedom with others in our churches. I recommend Henry Cloud and John Townsend's bestseller *Boundaries* for better understanding.[13]

- *Lighten up and laugh more often* (not at others' expense, though). Current research on how humor affects leadership has discovered that the most effective leaders use humor more often than less effective ones.[14]
- *Build relationships with no ministry purpose in mind.* Eugene Peterson said, "Pastors can lose touch with relational vitality when their relationships are driven by programmatic necessity. When this happens, pastors can lose the context for love, hope, faith, touch, and a kind of mutual vulnerability. In the midst of the congregation, pastors become lonely and feel isolated—and that isolation can be deadly to the pastoral life. Those are the conditions in which inappropriate intimacies flourish."[15]
- *Take care of your body* through exercise, healthy eating, and adequate sleep.
- *Master technology—don't let it master you.* I'm a techno geek. I was one of the original Mac owners and have an iPhone. I'm on Facebook; I tweet, text, e-mail, blog; I love electronic gadgets. I found, however, that technology was enslaving me. So I often don't check e-mail or CNN until after lunch on days when I have reserved the mornings for study or writing. This frees my mind and helps me focus on important tasks at hand rather than on returning the latest message or thinking about current world events. (Research has shown that the average worker is interrupted every eleven minutes and takes twenty-five minutes to refocus back on his job.[16] I found that to be generally true in my life when I compulsively checked e-mail.)
- *Periodically take a solo retreat.* Once every three months I spend a night and a day at a local retreat center. I'm usually the only one there. When I go, I think, pray, plan, write, and study. Those periodic getaways refresh my soul and help break me from the rigors of ministry, resetting my focus to respond appropriately to potential ministry killers.

Henri Nouwen taught in several universities before becoming pastor of a mentally handicapped community called Daybreak. After his vocational change, he wrote a book about leadership; *In the Name of Jesus* describes how his interaction at Daybreak became the most important experience of his life. What he learned shows what can happen when we *Show Up* with Integrity.

> *These broken, wounded, and completely unpretentious people forced me to let go of my relevant self—the self that can do things, show things, prove things, build things—and forced me to reclaim that unadorned self in which I am completely vulnerable, open to receive and give love regardless of any accomplishments.*[17]

In community at Daybreak, Nouwen "came to see that [he] had lived most of [his] life as a tightrope artist trying to walk on a high, thin cable from one tower to the other, always waiting for the applause when [he] had not fallen off and broken [his] leg."[18] He wisely noted that many of us feel like a failed tightrope walker because we've discovered we don't have what it takes to draw thousands.

I experienced this insight through four trips to Nicaragua. The church I serve recently adopted two ministries in its capital city, Managua. Earlier I mentioned my experience with Maria.

On my first trip, a furniture store owner from North Carolina hosted us. In Managua, Perry has built a compound that includes a church, a school, a feeding station, and a clinic. He drove me and a fellow pastor around during the day, and at night we slept in a mission home about forty minutes away.

One time Perry got permission from the parents of a ten-year-old girl, Catherina, to bring her back to the mission overnight. On our drive, I listened to Catherina talk in Spanish to one of our team members. Although my Spanish vocabulary is limited to the basic essentials (*taco, burrito*, and *enchilada*), I marveled at how well this girl articulated. Her intelligence seemed beyond her age.

She captured my heart. Through translation I learned that Catherina had an absentee dad, that she daily walked thirty minutes to school each way, and that her school didn't have enough books for everyone. Although she excelled beyond all the other students, she went home with no books. After learning her story, I knew what I had to do.

The next day our team, along with Catherina, spent two hours driving Managua's streets until we found a bookstore. With great joy for both of us, she picked out several books, pens, pencils, and other supplies to last her the year. That simple gesture knit our hearts together. Now each time I return and we drive into the compound, an olive-skinned girl with silky hair and almond eyes waits for me. During my last visit, as I stepped off the bus, she sprinted toward me. I scooped her up in my arms and as I swung her in circles I exclaimed, "Catherina! Catherina! Catherina!"

Even with our language barrier, she often clings to my side when I visit. My presence nourishes her soul. I know about which Nouwen speaks when he describes vulnerability and the freedom to give and receive love regardless of accomplishment. As God weans me from letting organizational frustrations hammer me, I'm slowly learning to focus on what matters most to His heart: love for Him and love for others.

Questions to Ponder

1. How would you respond if someone asked you, "Do you want to be worshiped?"
2. Mull over the definition of *integrity*. How full of integrity would others say you are?
3. Have you ever taken any of the inventories I suggested? If you have, find them and review them again. Do any insights surface after reading this chapter? If you've not taken any, what first step should you take now so you can take at least one in the next week?

CHAPTER 10

SPEAK UP WITH COURAGE (IS WHAT I WANT REALLY WHAT I NEED, AND WHO NEEDS TO KNOW?)

Sometimes, struggles are exactly what we need in our life. If we were to go through life without any obstacles, we would be crippled. We would not be as strong as what we could have been. Give every opportunity a chance. Leave no room for regret.[1]

—Author unknown

As I researched for this book, I received many stories from pastors who described the heartaches they've experienced in their churches. Although I've faced lots of challenges, mine seem anemic compared to what typifies many of theirs.

When "Pastor Larry" arrived in his first church, he quickly realized many there were at odds with one another. As he delicately navigated the issues, he began an outreach to children in the community, and he hired a church member as a part-time worker for this ministry.

She began to collect surveys that evaluated how the church felt about

Larry, and at one point he asked to see them because he'd heard that several made sharp criticisms about him and his wife. The woman refused. He then called a meeting with other layleaders to discuss the matter; emotions escalated to a crisis before the woman's father-in-law blurted, "You won't be able to get to your car before I beat you up!"

Fortunately, Larry was fast enough, and he arrived home intact. But this whole series of events reflected the church's deep spiritual sickness. Larry later left; he said it took two more churches and six years to rekindle his fire for ministry.

At another church, as "Pastor Betty" made her way through her first week, a woman visited her office and asked what day of the week they would begin to have lunch together. A bit surprised at the woman's forwardness, Betty asked why she wanted to do this so often and was told, "The previous pastor and I ate lunch together every week."

Betty replied that it would work best if they could meet on an as-needed basis. Unfortunately, this incited years of problems; the woman wielded great influence in the church as a leader in six key ministries, and she served as the treasurer. She began to criticize and undermine the pastor every chance she got. Betty later discovered that in almost every conversation, in any setting, her vitriol toward the pastor would surface.

The final straw came when the woman set up the church's bank account so that only she could access the financial records. The church ultimately consulted a lawyer, and although over time this treasurer was relieved of all her duties, she remained in the church and her unchanged attitude took a huge toll on Betty.

Betty described her pain in this way.

> *I have prayed for her. I have lost much sleep over her. I have tried to see her through Jesus' eyes. I have tried to not bring up her name in any*

conversation, but she has become the central focus of everything that is going on here at the church. I have allowed her to have great power over my peace. I am attempting to get by this. It is difficult.

I am still here as pastor, and the church asked me to return again. This year I will begin my seventh here, if I'm still alive!

Some days this feels like the end of the world. Other days I cope very well.

Thanks for listening.

Other excerpted snippets:[2]

- One member showed his disdain for the pastor in this way: He sung in the choir each Sunday yet would keep his head bowed the entire time the pastor preached. The whole church noticed his overt rejection during every service.
- A few families in one pastor's church were deeply committed to a para-church organization. They became extremely critical "of anything and everything that did not match up with their spiritual guru." These families believed the para-church teacher had a special connection with God and biblical understanding that the pastor lacked.
- Another pastor discovered that a disgruntled member (a founder and the church's biggest giver) had sent a critical letter to several hundred families, accusing the pastor of unbiblical teaching and questioning his leadership. It took several months to unravel the damage. Fortunately they avoided a split.
- At one church the leadership paid the pastor such a low salary that he had to shoot rabbits in his backyard to have meat for his family to eat. Ironically, the same church was about to pay off its debt and become debt free.

"As We Love Ourselves"

You may not have to shoot bunny rabbits to feed your kids, but I've found that all pastoral frustrations are relative. Whether large or small, they can hurt, distract, and rob our joy. I've suggested a four-part process that, when adapted to our specific settings, can help us best honor God as we deal with those issues.

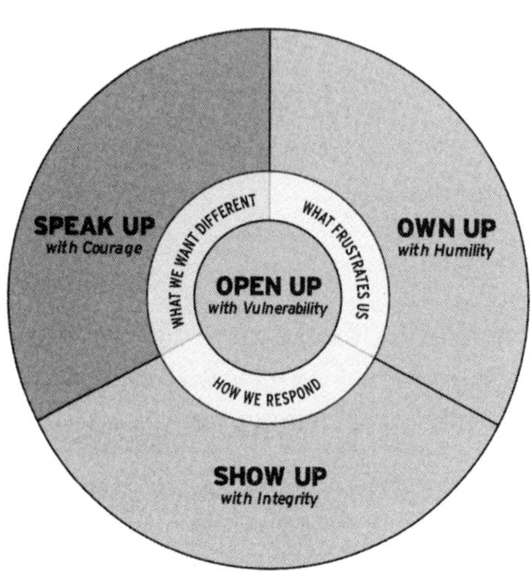

Thus far we've covered the first three parts. Central to a pastor's ability to process and manage his frustrations is *Opening Up* with Vulnerability. We all need safe people with whom we can talk.

Second, *Owning Up* with Humility involves honestly admitting what frustrates us and then, with God's help, reordering our frustrations to align with His priorities.

Third, *Showing Up* with Integrity means we evaluate what we do in response to those frustrations and then change the unhealthy responses to healthy ones.

Finally, *Speaking Up* with Courage suggests we discover the changes we believe will bring us greater joy and increased effectiveness. After this discovery, we determine who needs to know and how we should communicate the knowledge. This entire process is meant to help us defeat potential ministry killers.

Think back to the stories above. How should a pastor respond in similar circumstances? Just swallow hard, be happy, love Jesus, and turn the other cheek? Or do we consider that we have legitimate needs? If so, what are they? Are we selfish if we admit them to ourselves or to others? Dare we ask people in the church to meet them? Can we ask without appearing self-serving? If we do ask, have we compromised our call or our values? Have we contradicted the following Scriptures?

If anyone would come after me, he must deny himself and take up his cross and follow me.[3]

If anyone comes to me and does not hate his father and mother, his wife and children, his brothers and sisters—yes, even his own life—he cannot be my disciple.[4]

Care for the flock that God has entrusted to you. Watch over it willingly, not grudgingly—not for what you will get out of it, but because you are eager to serve God.[5]

If your first concern is to look after yourself, you'll never find yourself. But if you forget about yourself and look to me, you'll find both yourself and me.[6]

Deny yourself.
Hate your own life.
Don't serve grudgingly.
Forget about yourself.

When we couple these words with a pastor's call to selflessly serve God and others, we might conclude that if we think about ourselves, want our personal needs met, or desire that those we serve meet those needs, ministry has become all about us. So where does appropriate self-care end and self-centeredness begin?

I touched on this issue in chapter 6, when I described the Mutual Giving Cycle. Now I want to expand on how we can distinguish legitimate needs from illegitimate ones. Because God gave us legitimate needs, we must carefully and tactfully communicate them to the appropriate people either inside or outside our churches.

My maternal grandmother lived in Oak Park, a one-traffic-light town in southern Georgia. I remember our annual summer visits to see Granny Findley. My dad drove us in our baby blue '60s Dodge with plastic-covered seats and no air-conditioning. On the last leg, three miles down a dusty, unpaved road, our excitement would grow. As we pulled up to Granny's picket fence and my dad honked the horn, she'd always walk out on the porch to greet us, wearing her apron and bonnet.

My sister and I would hop out and dash up the wooden stairs to hug her; she always smelled like fried corn bread (a Southern delicacy). Then we'd make a beeline to the kitchen to find a snack and get a drink. Although her home had electricity, it lacked running water. That meant an outhouse for a bathroom, sponge baths in a galvanized tub on the back porch, and well water.

Granny usually tapped me to draw water from the well and fill the common bucket that rested on a small table in the kitchen. This provided our only source of drinking water. When we got thirsty we'd drink from an aluminum ladle that hung on the side of the bucket. Each time we scooped, the level would drop a bit, until finally I'd need to refill it again.

A pastor's capacity to serve and lead is like that bucket with the scoop. As we serve others, we scoop out and give people a portion of our limited emotions, time, and energy. Just as I had to regularly draw water from the well, we too must refill and replenish. When we don't fill our "buckets," ministry frustrations loom larger than reality and can more easily become ministry killers. We can also begin to give our greatest energies to those issues that seem most pressing but in reality aren't the most important.

Although many good leadership books encourage body care and time management to help fill our buckets, I won't focus on those here. Rather, I want to examine a bucket-filling aspect about which Paul wrote.

He counsels us to *carry each other's burdens.*[7] Clearly we are responsible *to* others, to help meet their needs and serve them. That's what we pastors do. Paul also clarifies those needs, however, with *"each one should carry his own load."*[8]

While we must serve others, they must carry their own share of the load. That God doesn't expect us to carry everybody else's responsibilities is reflected in the difference in the meanings of these two words. When the Greeks used *burden,* they meant something that could crush us or "break our back." Certainly we should help those who face struggles they can't bear alone. In contrast, *load* means daily-life responsibilities each of us should carry. When pastors take on loads *and* burdens, we deplete our buckets and trouble follows. We become more vulnerable to burnout, loss of joy, and even moral compromise.

Jesus himself often replenished his bucket. He set boundaries. He didn't heal every sick person. He didn't teach at every opportunity. When He got hungry He ate. When He got sleepy He slept. When He needed to admonish He did. When He needed to show compassion He did. To replenish, He often withdrew to spend time alone with His heavenly Father. Once ministry got so hectic He told His disciples to "Come with me by yourselves to a quiet place and get some rest."[9] Even in the Great Commandment Jesus compels us to "love your neighbor as *yourself.*"[10] Unless we replenish, we can't love others as we should because we haven't loved ourselves.

Pastor, we are not selfish when we appropriately take care of ourselves, establish healthy emotional and physical boundaries, own what we should and no more, and gracefully communicate our needs to others.

> *Don't boundaries turn us from other-centeredness to self-centeredness? The answer is no. Appropriate boundaries actually increase our ability to care about others. People with highly developed limits are the most caring people on earth.*[11]

In *Mad Church Disease,* Anne Jackson says,

> *When we create boundaries, we aren't saying to the world, "I can't help you." Instead, we're saying, "I must focus intentionally on the specific things God has placed right now in my direct influence." By saying no to people and to things that are not contained within God's distinct vision for our lives, we're actually saying "yes" to his sovereignty. He*

knows the best way for His will to be accomplished. For us to assume we can handle more is rebellious and counterproductive.[12]

So how can we separate our legitimate needs from unhealthy ones? What should we realistically expect from those we serve?

Here is a list of what pastors either said would bring them more joy or did bring them more joy in ministry:[13]

- I would like you [people in my church] to become more involved, attend more consistently, and become more committed to the church.
- I would like you to volunteer more, take on more ownership/leadership, and use your spiritual gifts.
- I would like you to become more consistent in your walk with Christ through such things as obedience, prayer, Bible reading, community involvement, and small-group involvement.
- I would like you to more often share your faith and invite people to church.
- I would like you to get along better with others, be more loving and encouraging to others, and forgive others more consistently.
- I would like you to be more open to new ideas, respect and support leadership more, complain/criticize less, and trust me more as your leader.
- I'd like you to accept me, try to understand me, and show that you personally care for me.
- I'd like you to pray for me more often.
- I'd like you to tell me that my ministry and teaching is making a difference in your life.
- I'd like you to show me more appreciation through simple gestures like notes, calls, or tangible tokens.
- I would like you to minister more to my wife and family.

Read through this list again and quickly circle three or four statements you believe describe your greatest desires. Now carefully review those and ask yourself in which category you'd place each: church/organizational, spiritual growth, relational health. If you found that most choices fell in the church/organizational category, you may not have picked true needs but valid desires. Remember, although we can't ignore organizational issues, God would rather we focus primarily on what's nearest to His heart—loving Him and others more and teaching those we serve to do the same.

Take time to wrestle with what you deeply believe would make ministry more fulfilling. Invite your safe person into that analysis. I've already admitted that at times I struggle too much with one particular organizational issue—attendance. I tend to think that if our church would just hit the next growth level, I'd find ministry more fun and engaging.

I'm a slow learner. When I started a church in Atlanta, I believed the magic attendance number would be 100. When we reached 100, it was 250. At 250 that still didn't satisfy, and I was convinced if we hit 500 I'd be happy as a clam. Attendance exceeded 500, but it never seemed enough. A thousand became the new magic number. The church I now serve averages a bit more than that every Sunday. But now the number I look for is 2,500. At Christmas and Easter attendance often exceeds that figure.

I recall my drive home a couple of years ago after the last of our five Christmas services. We had broken all previous records. I should have felt great, right? I didn't. I felt sad. As I wondered why, I realized my sadness rose from deep disappointment. I was glad we did so well, but victory seemed hollow. I thought a great attendance would magically quench my thirst for this *something* I wanted, but it didn't.

I'm discovering that what I think will fulfill me (organizational success) often comes up short. Now, I don't want to convey that I'm down on a growing church. The Great Commission commands us to reach as many people as we can, and that does imply numerical growth. But I'm convinced that organizational success and inner fulfillment will come as a by-product when we focus most on reaching the lost and the spiritual transformation and relational health of those currently in our churches.

When you've discovered what you believe are your valid needs, what next? You must own your legitimate responsibilities. We can't make people attend more often, give more money, or volunteer more consistently. We can't control whether a family tithes. "Guilting" people into biblical behavior may work for a while but not for long. Ultimately, every person makes his own choices.

However, we can teach what God wants. We can admonish and encourage when appropriate. We can pray for changed hearts. And we most definitely can and should communicate our valid needs to those who need to hear them.

How should we communicate our needs, and to whom? By now you've discovered what you believe are your true needs. Hopefully you've received insight from your safe friend as well. If you feel comfortable enough with your choices, consider one or more of the following suggestions to let others know what they are. It will take courage to speak up. And we can't demand that others meet them, but we are well within appropriate boundaries to make them known and then to trust God that people get the message and respond.

Tell Your Church

Eugene Peterson served the same church for twenty-nine years. During that time he clearly and graciously communicated his needs to his church by telling them this:

> *Help me. I have needs. I can't function well without help from you. We're in this together, we're doing the same thing, we're worshiping*

> *together, we're living the Christian life together. You've asked me to do certain things to help you do it—to lead you in worship on Sunday, to visit you when you're sick, to help administer the church. But I need help in all of this.* [14]

Peterson also wrote congregational letters four times a year on aspects of a pastor's life, such as why he keeps a Sabbath, why he reads books, and why he stays home on Friday nights.

The journalist who conducted the interview from which the above quote came made this observation: "It sounds as though you are not going to hold a congregation responsible for what is your responsibility. At the same time, you won't let them hold you responsible for what is their responsibility." In response, Peterson explained that he sought to create an environment that led to mutuality rather than an adversarial position. In doing so, "People feel that they're being valued for their own sake, not for what you can get out of them or how you can use them."[15] That's how we prioritize others' spiritual and relational needs over the church's organizational needs. People can usually sense the difference between a genuine request for help and a self-serving request.

Honesty and vulnerability can often endear us to others and at the same time bring us inner freedom. Craig Groeschel said that during his early years he performed well as a good pastor, yet something was missing in his life. One Sunday, after another good performance, God convicted him that he was often living a lie, not due to gross unconfessed sin, but because he attempted to project to others someone he wasn't.

With great courage, the next Sunday he stood before his congregation and bared his soul:

> *"My relationship with God is not what it should be." (My voice quavered. No one moved. I plunged ahead.) "I've confessed to God, but now I'm going to confess to you: I've become a full-time minister but a part-time follower of Christ."*[16]

The silence was so great immediately afterward that, he said, "You could have heard a Communion wafer snap." At that moment he changed, becoming "a full-time follower of Christ who happened to be a pastor."

Maybe you need to give a sermon on the life of a pastor in which you tactfully share some of your struggles, blind spots, and needs. Use this book as your permission to do so. Tell your church you just read a book about what pastors said were their greatest frustrations and what they'd like different from their church. Say the author suggested that bringing a message on this issue could help you become a better leader. Share the top six ways one of the surveys discovered how people in churches have encouraged their pastors (summarized here):

- You showed me tangible appreciation.
- You let me know that I spiritually impacted your life.
- You prayed for me.
- You accepted and understood me, cared for me, and were there when I needed you.
- You supported my leadership, defended me, and trusted me.
- You ministered to my wife and/or my family.

If you bring such a message, create a PowerPoint or a handout with this list. In doing so, you may plant heart-seeds that will later bear fruit. Give specific examples of when someone in your church encouraged you. Periodically sprinkle such experiences into your preaching.

People won't know what might encourage us unless we tell them, in the right spirit. Appeal to your church, as Eugene Peterson graciously did to his. Paul exhorted Timothy: "Preach the word of God. Be prepared, whether the time is favorable or not. Patiently correct, rebuke, and encourage your people with good teaching."[17]

One caution: Avoid pulpit revenge. When someone in our church angers or hurts us, we're tempted to lash out through a sermon. Once when a woman acted like a baby in response to something I did, I got so angry at her behavior that I crafted an entire message on why we need to show each other more grace. I wanted to make sure she got the message.

The Sunday morning I planned to preach it, I was pumped. I passionately preached, although of course I never mentioned her name. I would have felt quite proud about my admonishment except for one small detail: She didn't come to church that day. In retrospect I'm glad, because I probably would have made the situation worse.

Tell Your Board

Your church probably has some sort of board to whom you are ultimately responsible. In my case, elders are responsible to make sure our church stays true to its mission, theology, and goals. They also provide accountability to me. If any group should know how best to meet our needs, it would be that group.

However, I'm not so naïve as to overlook that some pastors' greatest frustrations come from those on their boards. If yours causes you the greatest headache, tread carefully with them as you communicate what you'd like done differently. Perhaps asking each member to read this book first might soften their hearts for such a conversation.

If you're on good terms with your board, share your needs at the appropriate time. Unless one of them has served in full-time vocational ministry, they really won't know what our world is like without our telling them. I faced a conflict with one of our elders on this very thing. He assumed he knew what I was up against on a daily basis, and I firmly told him he hadn't a clue. He disagreed at the time, but after reflection admitted that he didn't truly understand my world. I believe that experience helped open the door to bring about an eventual solution to the ongoing issue I faced with the elders (mentioned previously).

If our board knows what our needs are, they can help craft how we communicate those needs to the church. If this group takes their role seriously and truly cares about you, they should be your best allies in helping to meet your needs so you can most effectively serve and lead.

Tell Your Staff

We don't have a huge pastoral staff, but we begin our weekly meetings by sharing what happened in our world the week prior. Most weeks we share the normal stuff of life. Sometimes, however, another pastor will share a real burden or need. Sometimes I do as well. Those deeper conversations bind us closer together as co-laborers and help us meet each other's needs. Depending on your staff's spiritual maturity, let them into your world by verbalizing your needs. Don't keep them guessing. In addition to sharing with them, I also teach a yearly lesson that spells out the values I expect modeled in our church and on the job.

Tell Your Spouse

Although I've not addressed how crucial healthy marriages are to ministry, every pastor must make his or her marriage a priority. Sherryl knows my ministry world well and recently started working at our church. Our spouses should know our frustrations and needs, even though they may not be able to meet the needs that others in the church should meet.[18]

Tell Your Encouragers

Even though broken, hurting, and frustrating people fill our churches, I believe God has planted at least one encourager in yours. Read the verses below and note the common theme in each.

They refreshed my spirit and yours also. Such men deserve recognition.[19]

By all this we are encouraged. In addition to our own encouragement, we were especially delighted to see how happy Titus was, because his spirit has been refreshed by all of you.[20]

May the Lord show mercy to the household of Onesiphorus, because he often refreshed me and was not ashamed of my chains.[21]

Your love has given me great joy and encouragement, because you, brother, have refreshed the hearts of the saints.[22]

Paul repeatedly mentions someone who *refreshed* another's spirit. The root word conveys the idea of stopping, pausing, or resting. Jesus used it when He said, "Come to me, all you who are weary and burdened, and I will give you rest."[23] When someone refreshes our spirit, it helps pause, at least for a moment, the mental and emotional drain ministry brings.

Take a moment and picture in your mind those in your church who refresh your spirit. Perhaps they share a positive comment after a service. Maybe they send you notes or e-mails of appreciation. Or they may actually remember Pastor Appreciation Month. They might faithfully serve week in and week out. Thank them for their service and let them know you appreciate it when they appreciate you. Tell them personally. Give them a call. Send them a note or an e-mail.

Every Sunday I see myself as a cheerleader. I walk the halls of our building and thank those who serve that day. On Mondays, I send two or three e-mails to those who went over and above in their service. I also send notes of thanks to faithful givers. When people know we appreciate them, they will see us more favorably and, I believe, will be more open to God's prompting them to meet our needs.

Of course, our ultimate motivation to show appreciation should not be to get appreciation back. The deposits we place in others' souls, however, always come back to nourish ours. Find the encouragers in your church and let them know how much you appreciate them; you will find they'll either intentionally or unintentionally give back to you. Although Jesus was speaking primarily about money, His words imply the principle that we get what we give:

> *Give away your life; you'll find life given back, but not merely given back—given back with bonus and blessing. Giving, not getting, is the way.*[24]

Tell the People to Whom You'd Like to Say "I'd Be Better Off If I Never Saw Your Face in Church Again."

This suggestion may seem odd, but it might help minimize the grief you get from adversaries. You probably can conjure up with ease the names of those who frustrate you most. In some cases, investing relational time with them might lessen the angst you feel. At a minimum, consider asking some of those people to pray for you. You don't have to bare your soul, but if occasionally you share a few prayer needs, their hearts might soften toward you. I've found that when I pray for others toward whom I have a bad attitude, it's difficult for me to keep that attitude. Depending on the person, it might help to meet with him and suggest a few ways he could help you become a more effective leader. Such a conversation could resolve some of the pressing issues.

This chapter completes the suggested four steps that can help us process our frustrations: *Open Up* (with vulnerability), *Own Up* (with humility), *Show Up* (with integrity), and *Speak Up* (with courage). Before the wrap-up chapter, I've included one that speaks directly to the unique frustrations and ministry killers many pastors' spouses experience. I encourage both you and your spouse to read it.

Questions to Ponder

1. Does the thought of sharing how others might help meet your needs as a pastor make you feel uncomfortable? Why or why not?
2. How do you "replenish your bucket" successfully? If you can't think of ways, what activity could you begin that might help you do so?
3. What did you circle from the list of what pastors indicated they want to be different? Who should be the first person or group to begin discussing these needs? How can you go about it?

PART IV

"*CARPE DIEM.* SEIZE THE DAY, BOYS. MAKE YOUR LIVES EXTRAORDINARY."

CHAPTER 11

SPOUSE KILLERS

> *The pastor's wife is the only woman I know who is asked to work full time without pay on her husband's job, in a role no one has yet defined.*[1]
>
> —Ruthe White

In 1989, Robin Williams played the character John Keating in the film *Dead Poet's Society*. A charismatic English teacher with a passion for poetry and literature, he didn't endear himself to his school's administration, but he did to his students. On the first day, to encourage them to live life to the fullest, he displayed his unorthodox teaching methods. He took his boys out into the hallway to show them photos of past scholars he said were now "fertilizing daffodils." To emphasize his point, he brought them close to the photos and whispered into their ears this now famous movie quote: "*Carpe diem*. Seize the day, boys. Make your lives extraordinary."

I've given this final section that name because I believe it captures what I hope to leave with you. King David's words add an exclamation point: "This is the day the Lord has made; let us rejoice and be glad in it."[2] God has given every pastor this day, today, as a gift both to enjoy and to use for His glory. The more consistently we open up to safe people, own our issues, respond to them with integrity, and appropriately share our needs with others, the more we will truly rejoice in the ministry He has given us.

I've included this chapter in this section because *if we don't understand the potential ministry killers our wives face, we will hinder our effectiveness.* If we don't address the issues that siphon the life from our wives and try to help them, those killers may stifle the work God wants to do through both of you. These factors are more pervasive than we might think. One survey discovered that 85 percent of pastors' wives feel unprepared for the ministry lifestyle.[3] Another, by the Global Pastors Wives Network, found that "eight in ten pastors' wives say they feel unappreciated or unaccepted by their husband's congregations." Most shocking was their discovery that pastors' wives' issues are the number one reason pastors leave their ministries.[4]

Between You and Me

Sherryl and I married over thirty years ago. It all started with green beans.

We began seminary in Texas the same semester. We'd never met until that eventful day in the Buddy's Winn-Dixie grocery store. I'm known to get hyper-vigilant sometimes when it comes to spending money—I don't like to do it except to invest in life essentials (like Macs, iPhones, and Hi-Intensity LED flashlights). One of my first tasks upon moving to Fort Worth was to visit all nearby grocery stores to create a "best price" spreadsheet. With clipboard in hand, I surveyed five and discovered which had the cheapest prices on food like chicken, spaghetti, green beans, and bananas.

Buddy's, on Seminary Drive, carried the lowest prices on store-brand canned goods, and on that day my roommate and I were there to purchase the cheapest items. As we turned down the canned vegetable aisle, my cart magically pulled me toward another, halfway down, whose "driver" was the cutest girl I'd ever seen. Our carts bumped, sparks flew, and I fell in love.

I didn't want to overdo my attraction to this beautiful woman, so we chitchatted at first. After about ten seconds of small talk I asked for her address. She reluctantly gave it to me. I later discovered it was the wrong one. The rest is history.

In the last three decades we've faced many difficult challenges that, without Christ, long ago would have split us up. Although earlier I mentioned some of these, here again is a brief summary for context.

- During her adolescence, our oldest daughter rebelled for five hellish years. As a result, we sent her to seven different troubled-teen programs in four different states, had her arrested twice, and consulted almost twenty different counselors. She eventually returned to her faith and family. I chronicled our journey in a book.
- Just after our youngest daughter's first birthday, a tumor was discovered, growing deep inside her brain. In the last twenty-two years she's endured three different surgeries on her left arm and four different brain surgeries, including an experimental brain implant. We still pursue healing for her.
- When my wife was pregnant with our third child, we started a church in Atlanta with no people, no money, a gas credit card, and a friend's commitment to support us for six months at $100 per month.
- During the early years of our church start, Sherryl faced major surgery, her mother died, she took care of three active preschoolers, and my self-identity took a beating because this church looked like it was going to fail. I was not a very pleasant person to be around during those days.

I list these experiences not to elicit sympathy but to provide enough back-story to indicate that we've faced a lot, yet God's grace has sustained us. His grace can sustain you as well, no matter what you face.

In the next few pages my wife and I dialogue about pastors' spouses and ministry killers. Listen in as we talk. Look for common threads your wife or husband may experience.

Charles: I was shocked at the responses I *didn't* see from over a thousand pastors in the LifeWay study. Responding to "Please briefly describe what the people in your church could do differently to make your ministry in your church more joyful for you," only *one* (one!) pastor mentioned his wife. (He said one way the church could make ministry more joyful would be to "recognize the contributions of his wife.")

I'm not sure what to make of the lack of reference to spouses. But it seems to imply that some pastors either are oblivious to those struggles or don't believe their wife's struggles significantly impact their own leadership effectiveness.

From your perspective, Sherryl, do wives face their own ministry killers? Do they deal with issues that can drain the life out of their souls and in turn negatively affect their husbands? If so, what killers do you believe pose the greatest risk to a pastor's wife?

Sherryl: Most definitely pastors' wives face painful ministry killers. I've experienced them, and the pastors' wives with whom I've dealt have as well. Although every church is different, if I listed issues that pose the greatest risk for a pastor's wife to withdraw, get hurt, or become bitter, these killers definitely would make the cut.

1. Deep loneliness
2. Inescapable vulnerability with others

3. Living in a fishbowl world
4. Managing unrealistic and unfair expectations
5. Having little or no voice in response to church decisions or to church critics

Charles: That sounds even tougher than what we pastors face. We've often discussed that ministry requires that we spend lots of time with people. But you mention loneliness at the top. What do you mean by that?

Sherryl: When you and I married, transitioning into being a pastor's wife was pretty smooth for me. Since we were both enrolled in seminary, and you were part-time in a local church, we'd built many friendships. So it seemed easy. That is, until two years later when we moved to another state as you took your first full-time job. That's when the reality of being a pastor's wife hit home.

In our new church I experienced something I'd never felt before. People were nice to me, but they didn't want me to be a part of their lives. I kept wondering why I couldn't "click" with these people. I continued to invite families over for dinner and have play dates with other moms and their kids. But an incredible loneliness began to envelop me. We were hundreds of miles from our families. And because I'm an outgoing person, I wondered why I couldn't find the friendships I needed for emotional support.

I'll never forget one Sunday in that new church when I first visited the young-married adult class. You had other responsibilities that morning so I went alone. As people gathered in little groups to talk before the class, I went from group to group to introduce myself and tried to make friendly conversation. Often people would smile, nod their heads, and then drop the conversation. Several times they actually turned their backs on me in mid-conversation.

Unfortunately, this was not a onetime experience. Although some people were friendly, I felt an underlying current that they were distancing themselves from me. One Sunday I hurt so much I even had to fight back tears. I finally quit trying and volunteered to teach a class of five-year-olds. At least the kids liked me.

Through my experiences, my dialogue with other pastors' wives, and my own research, I've concluded this: A "loneliness void" is the most intense occupational hazard, or ministry killer, a pastor's wife will face. Many people in churches expect that she be almost perfect, or at least appear that way. This unspoken expectation often makes us feel very vulnerable because we think that if others see our faults, they will reject us.

On the other hand, many view us as not having real needs. Or, if they do, not the ones an average woman in the church feels she could help meet. Even when people know we're dealing with something difficult, sometimes they minimize the issue because they assume we're strong enough to handle it ourselves. *After all,* they may reason, *the pastor lives with you.* All of these misconceptions can leave us feeling alone and isolated.

Charles: I had forgotten you endured that pain when I began my first full-time position. I know that sometimes we pastors get so lost in our own worlds that we don't realize that you hurt too. How have you seen the demands on me affect this sense of loneliness?

Sherryl: Well, since you asked, I'll be frank. Sometimes your ministry obligations have contributed to my loneliness. Unlike many other professions, your job often requires that you attend early morning or evening meetings. Sometimes by the time you get home, you're too tired to be truly present for the kids and me. I know you want to be available, but you don't have the energy to muster what we need from you.

I've seen this come in cycles. For the most part you've done your best to be available. But when meetings go back-to-back for several evenings or you get mentally preoccupied with ministry concerns, I reason that the church needs you more than I do.

I've tried to suck it up and do double duty with home responsibilities so you'll be free for the ministry. Often when that happens, I don't feel you are there for me to confide in. The loneliness becomes even more acute.

In your research you interviewed several experts who work with pastors and their wives, and I recall these words from Russ Veenker:

> *Sometimes a pastor's wife feels that she must compete with the church for her husband's attention. It's almost like the church has become his mistress. She has to fight for his affections, and he often feels nagged. In those cases, pastors will often make such statements like, "I want my home to be my sanctuary," or "I want my home to be a place of rest." This results in over-commitment to the church, and his unavailability to her often leads to depression and disillusionment for both of them.*

Charles: I recall those conversations when you confronted me about my imbalance. I didn't like them, but I needed a jolt to get me back on track. And I believe Dr. Veenker correctly assessed this dynamic. When pastors add to their wives' loneliness through inadvertently making the church a mistress, both pastor and wife lose.

You chose vulnerability as the second killer on your list. Tell us more about that one.

Sherryl: Pastors' wives face a unique kind of vulnerability. By default, the church where her husband serves often becomes the center of her life in several areas. It's her main opportunity for service, the place to find some of her closest relationships, the source of her family's primary means of financial support, and her home away from home. Unfortunately, it also becomes the source of the greatest criticism. Unlike many women who find volunteer opportunities, friendships, and income through other various venues, a pastor's wife often finds all three wrapped up in the same place: the church.

This can become an example of the proverbial "eggs all in one basket." The history of the word *pastor* illustrates this idea. The Old English term for *person*, "parson," became commonly used to describe a pastor, because the man and the vocation were so integrated that they'd become synonymous. The same holds true for a pastor's wife.

A politician's wife comes closest to this predicament. She must guard what she says so that her words always reflect well on her husband. If she slips, what she says could become fodder for his opponents and could lead to controversy or defeat in a future election. One wife told me as we discussed church relationships, "You have to remember that the sharks are circling."

Current research has pinpointed how pastors' wives respond. Jama Davis noted in her doctoral dissertation[5] the same reaction I've seen in my conversations with pastors' wives. This vulnerability runs so deep that many wives are even reluctant to share their hurts with other pastors' wives in their own church or those in nearby churches. They don't feel safe even with their own kind. What could become an avenue for intimacy, prayer, and mutual encouragement is often perceived as a threat. As a result, pastors' wives tend to meet these needs through impersonal or anonymous venues, such as online communities, retreats with women they probably won't ever see again, and books.

Charles: Since you've had your share of loneliness and vulnerability, how have you dealt with this?

Sherryl: Well, over the years God has brought a few safe people into my life. Your chapter on finding a safe friend definitely applies to all pastors' wives. Fortunately, one of mine has been a professional counselor who was a preacher's kid. She understands my world both experientially and professionally. I would encourage pastors' wives to find a safe person, even if it's a professional counselor who understands ministry life. Professional coaching also could provide a source of help.

On a very personal note, the Lord has used the pain of ministry loneliness to draw me closer to Him. I often have meditated on Philippians 3:10: "I want to know Christ and the power of his resurrection and the fellowship of sharing in his sufferings." When I've done this, God reminds me that many situations in Jesus' life brought Him loneliness.

His family once thought he was mentally unstable. Judas betrayed Him. He experienced agony in the garden of Gethsemane. Peter denied Him three times. When I reflected on His experiences, I would often ask the Holy Spirit to help me empathize with His loneliness and betrayal.

As a result, He would comfort and encourage me. I began to see that through these lonely times He was allowing me to taste His sufferings. I realized Jesus doesn't ask me to bear something greater than what He bore. Rather, the "taste" lets me better understand His sacrifice for me. Because He promises never to leave us or forsake us, I know that I am not alone in my loneliness. Jesus understands.

At the same time I prayed to understand His loneliness, I also prayed He would bring friends who could help meet these needs in my life.

Charles: I've heard the "fishbowl" analogy before, and I think I get it. You listed it as your third killer. What exactly do you mean?

Sherryl: Let me illustrate this way: One Saturday afternoon I rode in the backseat as several of us returned from our church's women's retreat. As I mindlessly scanned the landscape, seemingly from nowhere a thought interrupted my daydreaming. *You are the most powerful woman in your church. You can make or break your husband's ministry.* My first reaction was, *What?* My second was, *Hmmm, that's right.* At first I wasn't sure if God or Satan gave me the thought, but it sure made me think.

As I continued to reflect, I recalled a pastor's wife who disliked being in ministry so much that she refused even to attend church. Her choice eventually led the pastor to leave the ministry. I knew another pastor's wife who had an affair with a man in the church. The pastor and his wife divorced, and he never returned to vocational ministry.

On the positive side, I've also known many pastors' wives who are indispensable to their husband's ministries, willingly serving alongside them in meaningful and complementary ways.

I determined early on that I would always try to add to rather than detract from your role as pastor. Although I really wanted to do this, I wasn't sure what it looked like. So in my early ministry years, I drew upon the examples I saw in two other older pastors' wives. I tried to imitate the way they supported their husbands in ministry.

With the Lord's strength I sought to become a Christian role model to the church by being a godly wife and mother. It wasn't as easy as the wives I tried to emulate made it appear. I never felt I was adequate to meet both the needs of the church and our family. I thought if I could just do more and be more then maybe I could become a shining role model, a combination of June Cleaver, Miss Congeniality, and Mother Teresa. On the other hand, I didn't want to appear inauthentic. The tension between meeting others' expectations and my own self-expectations began to weigh heavily on me.

Then a year after we began our church in Atlanta, we were devastated when we learned Tiffany had a brain tumor. Now not only did I feel pressured to be a role model, but our baby's survival also was at stake. It was too much. I finally gave up fitting someone else's mold. I threw out pretense as we desperately clung to our faith during that first surgery and the months of recovery and therapy. As each day we faced uncertainty with Tiffany, many church eyes were watching to see how we handled the crisis.

So when I say that a fishbowl experience can become a ministry killer for a pastor's wife, I mean this: We not only must face the normal and painful stuff life throws at us, but we must do it as the church looks on.

Fortunately, what created anxiety in the fishbowl also challenged me to deepen my walk with Christ. Knowing that others watched my response to crises spurred me to move forward in my faith rather than to wallow in self-pity. Had I not been in the fishbowl, I'm not sure I would have relied as much on His grace.

As I reflect on Jesus' life, I realize He revealed the Father's heart to us even when He lived in a fishbowl. The people expected Him to be one kind of Messiah, but He didn't meet their expectations. Instead, He met His Father's. He lived to please God, not others.

This understanding freed me. Although I can only reflect His image dimly, even in the fishbowl I want to mirror His character as clearly as possible. When I try to keep my eyes on the Lord to seek His approval, I'm more at peace and free to be me when I deal with others' expectations. As a pastor's wife I must remind myself that one day I will stand before Him to give an account of my life. Then the only thing that will matter is that my life reflected Him well.

Charles: I've always admired your deep desire to please God over all others. You've challenged my life in that area.

You also just mentioned "expectations," which is the fourth ministry killer you listed. What do you mean, specifically, and how have you seen pastors' wives respond?

Sherryl: The spoken and unspoken expectations churches place on pastors' wives landed on my list because every church has them. Most churches don't *officially* say they expect certain things from pastors' wives. However, they're as pervasive as dust bunnies and differ from what they expect from other women in the church. I'll explain what I mean by describing three ways I've seen pastors' wives respond.

Some pastors' wives simply give up when they can't meet the expectations. They withdraw and often sullenly sit alongside their husbands in church and do little else. One wife had been burned in the past yet looked forward to her husband's new church. As she planned a fresh start, she eagerly began to meet new people, sing solos, and even lead the annual women's retreat. She tried her best, but unfortunately careless words from others wounded her once again. Two years later when I saw her, I was astonished at her countenance. Once a vibrant, excited woman, full of life, she now stood listless next to her husband and looked sad, lonely, and isolated. She had retreated from most activities and chose instead to focus her energies on her career outside the church. Soon people began to quietly criticize the pastor because of her withdrawal. As soon as another church opened up, they moved.

Others yield to despair, helplessness, and hopelessness. I experienced this at a retreat I attended with fifty other pastors' wives. As each large-group session ended, the speaker asked us to complete the statement "I am tired of . . ." One young mother in the back blurted out, "Living!" A deafening silence filled the room as we craned our necks to see who had spoken. Later, when I reached out to her, she tearfully confided that she felt overwhelmed and overworked with her responsibilities at home and at church. She was afraid to resign from any of her church responsibilities because she believed it would hurt her husband and could even threaten his job security. She lived under guilt and despair.

At that retreat we later divided into small groups for discussion. One wife in my group confided that she was tired of living too but couldn't muster the courage to say it to everyone. Here is what she told our small group: "I have a pastor's wife mask I hang on my door that I put on when I go to church. Once I get home, I hang it up again." She felt she couldn't be herself at church. She feared that if she was, and people *knew* her, they'd reject her.

Others outright rebel. When they face continued pressures, some act out almost like teenagers. Some have turned to affairs. Others have left their husbands. Some have made statements simply to get a rise out of members. I knew one who had her body pierced and tattooed and deliberately wore clothing at church to prominently display her body art. Sometimes I've wondered if, on a subconscious level, these women hope that acting out might get their husbands (and themselves) kicked out. The prospect of being out from under these expectations may seem worth the loss of respect that would come from getting booted from the church.

I admit these responses are extreme, though they're more common than we think. But not every pastor's wife responds in these ways. Many move forward the best they can with grace and dignity. They pray, lean on the Lord, and seek encouragement from His Word. They seek out godly influences and help their husbands understand their struggles. I've certainly not managed expectations perfectly, but by God's grace the two of us have not yielded to these ministry killers.

Charles: I know how I feel when I face unrealistic expectations. At least I have some recourse to deal with them through my leadership teams. But your last ministry killer touches on something unique: *having little or no voice in response to church decisions or to church critics.* Unravel that one for us.

Sherryl: This issue concerns two groups: church boards and your critics. Boards where we've served have seldom asked for my thoughts on decisions. I recognize that because I don't serve on those boards they aren't bound to ask me what I think. And most decisions have had little direct bearing on our family or me. However, when a decision does impact our family, as a pastor's wife I'm not able to voice concerns for fear that such disapproval could affect your job or how others may perceive you.

As for critics, we've often felt the brunt of unfounded criticism through an e-mail, a call, or a conversation. It hurts, especially when it comes from someone we've thought safe.

It's easy for a pastor's wife to take offense. Since these criticisms aren't directed toward me, Matthew 18 instructs me not to bring them up; rather, you're the one who is to approach the critic. But because I'm your wife, when you get criticized, I feel criticized as well. To add insult to injury, I'm expected to be gracious when I come in contact with these people. This makes me feel bound and gagged.

I remember once when a couple came to talk to you. The wife had been hurt because she believed you ignored her by not speaking to her one Sunday morning. Even though you explained that your oversight was inadvertent and that you'd be more sensitive next time, they left the church a few months later. I struggle with those situations because I feel I have no voice. I feel powerless. I want to express my disappointment with such people and help them get perspective, but if they've already decided to leave, it profits little.

One of our most painful situations occurred when the board called a business meeting to let the church air its concerns about your leadership. At this meeting you were forced to defend yourself. You told me it might be best if I stayed at home to avoid more hurt. I decided to go anyway. In my attempt to cope with the powerlessness I felt, I dressed up in one of my nicest outfits. When I arrived, I marched down the aisle with my head held high and took a seat on the front row right next to you. That night everybody else was free to stand up and say anything they wanted. Yet I didn't feel that freedom. Perhaps I felt that way because I've never heard of any other pastor's wife doing so in a business meeting. Fortunately, things went well and all I got was a tension headache.

Charles: That was a tough night. I shudder when I think about it. I had forgotten how it affected you. I'm glad we haven't had to experience anything like that again.

As you've described this lack of voice, I'm reminded that although this is true, a pastor's wife still carries great weight because she usually has the ear of her husband.

Sherryl, you've described five pastors' wives' ministry killers. In summary, what advice would you give spouses that might help them navigate these inevitable challenges?

Sherryl: Charles, I'd like to suggest three ideas I've found helpful.

First, we must practice what I call "pre-forgiveness." Most wives will face at least some of these ministry killers. Disappointment, hurt, and discouragement come with ministry. Knowing this, I've tried to position my heart ahead of a hurt to extend grace even before it's needed.

Wounded women easily can become bitter. Scripture tells us that bitterness hurts not only us but also those around us. If my heart is filled with grace when someone throws a dart at me, God's grace can surround it before it can wound me. I've not always done this, but when I have, those hurts have not become places where bitterness could grow.

Second, we must use a trained counselor when we can't move forward from a hurt. I've found that some words and actions from church people act like triggers. They trigger feelings rooted in unresolved hurts we've brought from our past. I believe God actually allows this pain to prompt us to seek help from others so we can be free of our baggage. The pain reminds us that we've not yet moved beyond a past experience. Thus someone who hurt us actually can become a tool that God uses to grow us. Joseph's response to his brothers when he revealed himself to them demonstrates this: "You intended to harm me, but God intended it for good."[6]

Finally, as you and I have both mentioned, pastors' wives should find a trusted friend with whom they can walk through their valleys. Some wives may consider themselves strong enough to handle what ministry brings by drawing upon their own strength and the Lord's. But I believe the story of Lazarus challenges that thought.

After Lazarus had been in the tomb three days, Jesus arrived. As He looked at the tomb where Lazarus's body lay, He told Lazarus to come out. He truly performed an astonishing miracle in raising the dead.

Yet Jesus didn't do everything. He had someone else move the stone from the tomb. He instructed others to remove the graveclothes. We do need others to help us avoid being bound by the graveclothes of ministry killers.

I'd like to share one final thought. Although being a pastor's wife brings many challenges, my role allows for spiritual impact that few others experience. I'm able to invest in your life as few others can. I believe I make a unique contribution to the body of Christ expressed through the local church where we serve. Despite all the challenges I face, I wouldn't trade my role for any other. I hope the wives who read this would see themselves in the same way.

Charles: Sherryl, thanks for sharing your insight. This dialogue has reminded me that I must pay more attention to the issues unique to you. And I'd like to add one more thought to what you've said.

Although in chapter 7 I encourage pastors to find a safe friend, I imagine many of us place our wives in this role. You have been a wonderful sounding board when I've struggled in ministry. You truly are a safe friend. But I believe we must be careful about putting too much on our wives.

I also referred to the Pastors Institute, which created a scientifically valid inventory where pastors could self-assess themselves in five areas related to ministry: fulfillment, connectedness, proficiency, self-care, and non-church areas like family life and financial issues. Between May 2003 and January 2009, 1,086 pastors from forty-two denominations took the inventory. Some statistically significant findings shed light on our relationships with our wives.

From "connectedness," the good news is that pastors responded significantly higher to the statement "My spouse supports me in my ministry" than to any of the other nine statements in that category. This implies that pastors in general see their wives as their strongest supporters. The flip side is, we must be careful not to overload our wives with our frustrations.

Mark McMinn, former professor at Wheaton College, wrote:

> *A male pastor relying on his wife for support may function well most of the time, but this narrow support system will become a problem if*

she is not able to fulfill that role (if she herself becomes burned out, depressed, disabled, disillusioned, and so on).[7]

Pastors, we must heed this counsel. When our wives feel overloaded, we should lean more into our safe friends. And if you are a pastor's wife and feel overloaded by your own ministry killers, please talk to your husband and let him know how you feel. Unless he knows, he may inadvertently add to your stress.

Questions to Ponder

1. As a pastor's spouse, which of the five ministry killers affects you the most? How have you responded to it?
2. Again, as a pastor's spouse, is there one thing you would like to say to your spouse that you have not said?
3. What one practical step forward could you make this week that might deepen your appreciation of your role as a pastor's spouse?

CHAPTER 12

AFTER YOU SELL THE BOOK ON EBAY, WHAT'S NEXT?

> *Saint John of the Cross says that two purifications occur in the dark night of the soul. . . . The first involves stripping us of dependence upon exterior results. We find ourselves less and less impressed with the religion of the "big deal"—big buildings, big budgets, big productions, big miracles. Not that there is anything wrong with big things, but they are no longer what impresses us. Nor are we drawn toward praise and adulation. Not that there is anything wrong with kind and gracious remarks, but they are no longer what move us. . . .*[1]
>
> —Richard Foster

As I began this book, I shared about Maria, pastor of the church in the Managua, Nicaragua, city dump. My meeting with her and the subsequent meetings profoundly impacted my life. I use her as an example because although she faces incredible odds (what would be ministry killers for many pastors in America), she doesn't allow them to defeat her.

And Maria's response to those challenges isn't just a defensive posture to keep things from getting worse; she seems to thrive in her circumstances, looking beyond them with an elephant-sized vision. She now wants to build a ten-times-bigger church so she can expand the school, hold services for larger crowds, and begin a vocational school for teaching trades to those who live off the dump's garbage. She's already started a Bible school and a second church. In my last conversation with her, she said she believes God will bring revival to her country so that Nicaragua can be a tool in His hands to bring revival to the United States. *That's* vision!

Still, many dark nights of the soul have filled the last ten years of Maria's life. Every pastor faces unique ministry challenges and potential ministry killers. Some pastors, who are just entering the ministry, may have yet to face them. Some are in the throes of difficulty but see light at the end of the tunnel. And some may see no hope at all.

I pray that wherever you find yourself, this book will have encouraged you to stay the course. I've tried to present compelling research to accurately describe potential killers that frustrate us, how we respond to them, and what we'd like to be different. I've also suggested a process that can help us defeat those killers: *Open Up* with vulnerability, *Own Up* with humility, *Show Up* with integrity, and *Speak Up* with Courage.

During the several months I was writing this book, I faced quite a few pressing challenges in my ministry. The economy tanked, and we downsized our pastoral staff by two to make ends meet (and we didn't have a huge staff). Our elders and I wrestled with my leadership role. I struggled about my ministry's future. And I saw a professional to help me deal with the broken places in my heart that influenced all the issues above. Not surprisingly, writing became therapeutic for me.

In this process, I found many disparate quotes and ideas that didn't quite fit into any other chapter but still applied to the book's theme. So I parked them in a document that became the foundation for this last chapter. Many of the nuggets were quotes from others that struck a chord with me. I hope they encourage you as we seek to honor Christ through our calling as pastors.

Don't Try to Insulate Yourself From Pain

Pain and ministry go together like peanut butter and jelly. Once you make a PB&J sandwich, there's no separating the two ingredients. Neither can we isolate successful ministry from the pain it inevitably brings. I don't like rejection, disappointment, or criticism. I don't know any pastor who does. Sometimes, I do everything I can to avoid them.

A French nun, who lived in the late 1800s, Thérèse of Lisieux (known as "the Little Flower"), practiced a simple way to draw closer to Jesus:

> *It is, in short, to seek out the menial job, to welcome unjust criticisms, to befriend those who annoy us, to help those who are ungrateful.*[2]

Thérèse didn't allow those experiences to help her grow only if they happened to come her way; she actually sought them out and embraced them. As difficult as that seems, perhaps the Lord would want you to consider this unusual tool to help you become a more effective pastor and follower of Jesus.

Learn to Absorb Punches With Grace

This thought is a cousin to the previous insight. At some time in your ministry, someone has probably taken an intentional punch at you. I don't mean they punched you in the face, but they've likely taken a swipe at your leadership, preaching, or vision. It hurts. I believe the higher we go in leadership, the more punches we'll have to absorb. Abraham Lincoln, arguably our country's greatest president, took many punches, and his very words carry a timely message for us:

> *If I were to try to read, much less answer, all the attacks made on me, this shop might as well be closed for any other business. I do the very best I know how—the very best I can; and I mean to keep doing so*

> *until the end. If the end brings me out all right, what's said against me won't amount to anything. If the end brings me out wrong, ten angels swearing I was right would make no difference.*[3]

I might add to this thought what a close friend once told me. "Even when church problems aren't your fault, take the high road of grace and integrity as you respond to them."

Slow Your Pace of Ministry

Thomas Kelly, a twentieth-century Quaker, died the day a company discussed publishing his essays. Fortunately a friend followed through and those essays were compiled into *A Testament of Devotion*. Kelly succinctly captures why we need to heed Jesus' offer: "Come to me, all you who are weary and burdened, and I will give you rest."[4]

We live our lives in "an intolerable scramble of panting feverishness."[5] This easily can overtake us with the demands ministry brings. With sermons to prepare, plans to develop, people to disciple, and always, seemingly not enough time, I sometimes have to tell myself out loud, "*Slow down.*" When I'm caught up in a frenetic pace, ministry frustrations often loom larger than they really are.

Learn to Be Okay When Things Don't Go Your Way

Circumstances beyond our control (demographics or a location that hinders growth), an uncooperative board (they say no to an important initiative), or even family issues (a chronically ill child who requires an inordinate amount of energy) can hinder and dilute our ministry efforts. In other words, we seldom immediately see the benefit from brokenness.

Brokenness has touched my life in the two places where it hurts the most: my family (one chronically sick child, one who rebelled for five years) and my ministry (many dreams yet unfulfilled). But Jesus said brokenness must precede fruit bearing.

> *Truly, truly, I say to you, unless a grain of wheat falls into the earth and dies, it remains by itself alone; but if it dies, it bears much fruit.*[6]

The nineteenth-century Danish theologian Søren Kierkegaard said, "God creates everything out of nothing—and everything God is to use he first reduces to nothing."[7]

Richard Foster, one of today's most influential voices on spiritual formation, described one of the greatest benefits from brokenness. He calls this the "crucifixion of the will" and says it brings "freedom from the everlasting burden of always having to get our own way."[8] Having to always get our own way is the antithesis of the other-centered life Jesus modeled for us.

Make Spiritual Receptivity the Biggest Thing in Your Life

As I finished this chapter, I audited a doctoral course at Trinity Evangelical Divinity School, where I received my Doctor of Ministry. For an entire week we talked about prayer. Prior to that week I read several books on prayer, one of them a reread of Tozer's *The Pursuit of God*. In one place he observed how the great saints of old, whether biblical or post-biblical characters, vastly differed from each other:

> *How different, for example, was Moses from Isaiah; how different was Elijah from David; how unlike each other were John and Paul, St. Francis and Luther, Finney and Thomas à Kempis. The differences are as wide as human life itself—differences of race, nationality, education, temperament, habit and personal qualities. Yet they all walked, each in his day, upon a high road of spiritual living far above the common way.*[9]

Tozer then noted that they all had in common one vital quality: spiritual receptivity. They were open to God, and they cultivated this quality. They went one step beyond the steps most Christians take. Rather than simply feeling a longing for God, they acted upon it, as did King David when he penned this verse:

> *When my heart whispered, "Seek God,"*
> *my whole being replied, "I'm seeking him!"*[10]

Remember That Ultimately We Serve the People; They Don't Serve Us

F. B. Meyer, a Baptist contemporary and friend of D. L. Moody, authored over forty books. He understood that when God gives gifts to pastors, we are to humbly use them in service to Him and to others.

> *I used to think that God's gifts were on shelves one above the other and that the taller we grew in Christian character the more easily we could reach them. I now find that God's gifts are on shelves one beneath the other and that it is not a question of growing taller but of stooping lower.*[11]

This reminds me that the opportunities and gifts God gives us are not to build us up, but rather, as we humble ourselves, God will use them to build others up.

Do the Best You Can and Leave the Results to God

That phrase may seem a bit worn, but it's well worth heeding. In Christ's parable of the talents, the master, representing God, gave responsibility to the servants based on individual ability.[12] The story implies that some pastors have greater competencies than others. Similarly, Paul teaches that the Holy Spirit gives gifts as He sees fit.[13] It's obvious that the Spirit gives some pastors extra preaching or leading gifts, evidenced in the size and impact of their ministries.

It's easy to become discouraged when we do our best yet don't see our church grow like others to which we may compare ourselves. When we wrap our identities around numerical results and the numbers don't increase, the discouragement can overwhelm us. This is especially true for older pastors who realize they may never achieve the dreams they had for ministry.

David Goetz wrote,

> *I often sat in the studies of both small-church pastors and mega-church pastors, listening to their stories, their hopes, their plans for significance. I deduced, albeit unscientifically, that often clergymen in midlife had worse crises of limits than did other professionals. Religious professionals went into the ministry for the significance, to make an impact, called by God to make a difference with their lives. But when you're fifty-three and serving a congregation of 250, you know, finally, you'll never achieve the large-church immortality symbol, the glory that was promised to you. That can be a dark moment—or a dark couple of years.*[14]

However, noted theologian Fred Rogers, of *Mr. Rogers* fame, recalled an experience he had when attending seminary. He wanted to hear a variety of preachers, so for a time he visited a different church each Sunday. One week he experienced "the most poorly crafted sermon [he] had ever heard." A friend had accompanied him, and when he turned to her, he found her in tears. She said, "It was exactly what I needed to hear."

Rogers then told his audience, "That's when I realized that the space between someone doing the best he or she can and someone in need is holy ground. The Holy Spirit had transformed that feeble sermon for her—and as it turned out, for me too."[15] Although the results from our best efforts may look feeble to some, they can touch a heart and change a life when we least expect it. This side of heaven we will never know the people we impacted through our faithful service.

Intensify Personal Relationships

My type-A personality inclines me to pick tasks over people when given a choice. As a result, I can easily miss relational moments meant for kingdom impact. As I wrote this section, it was the last day in the office for Sue Robinson, our administrator who faithfully served our church over twelve years. She and her husband were both retiring and moving to Texas. I had scheduled several hours to write that day, and then I received a call from my wife saying the other admin staff had planned an impromptu pizza lunch as a going-away gesture.

When Sherryl asked if I were going, I got perturbed. We already threw a party three days prior, and we planned to recognize them both in the following Sunday's service. I was on a schedule to write, then cut the grass, then go to the chiropractor, and then help Sherryl prepare for a staff fellowship at our house that night.

I had programmed myself for maximum efficiency. *I* had needs that *I* needed to meet . . . to be efficient with *my* time and accomplish as much as possible that day (for Jesus, of course). As I reflected, though, on how Jesus would want me to respond, I chose to surrender my schedule for the good of others. While I didn't get to write as much as I wanted, my presence communicated to Sue that I truly cared. Relationships trumped the tyranny of the urgent; often, they should.

As we all battle the temptation to yield to ministry killers, I leave two final thoughts with you:

First, the apostle Paul, inarguably the most influential Christian who ever lived, made his impact for two reasons:[16] He *kept an eternal perspective*: "We do not lose heart. . . . We fix our eyes not on what is seen, but on what is unseen. For what is seen is temporary, but what is unseen is eternal."[17] And he *relied on an eternal power*: "To this end I labor, struggling with all his energy, which so powerfully works in me."[18] If we desire to impact the world for Christ, it behooves us to follow Paul's example.

Second, David Goetz deftly reveals the meaning of Paul's words in 2 Timothy 4.6: "As for me, my life has already been poured out as an offering to God."[19] He wrote, "I never really absorbed the implication of that verse until recently: You don't leave your mark on the world, you empty your mark *into* the world."[20]

I pray that God will use you mightily for His kingdom as you serve Him and empty your mark into the world.

Questions to Ponder

1. Which of the insights above is/are most difficult for you to apply in your life, and why? What would have to change in your life to make that insight more real?
2. What is the one takeaway from this book that impacted you the most?

APPENDIX

RESEARCH DETAILS

Study One

The Barna Group surveyed by phone 615 Protestant senior pastors in November 2007 in their annual PastorPoll using a CATI (Computer Assisted Telephone Interviewing) system that ensures the survey data are recorded properly. In research terminology, the cooperation rate was 93 percent, unusually high for such a study. This significantly raises confidence in the survey's findings. The sampling error was +/– four points.

The pastors surveyed came from within the forty-eight continental United States and represented a cross section of denominations, ages, church size, and tenure. This survey asked these three questions:

1. *For you, what are the types of issues that cause the most disappointments or frustrations between you and the people in your church?* (open-ended question)
2. *Consider the last year or so and the disappointments or frustrations*

you may have experienced with the people in your church. Which of the following best describes your experience? (closed-ended question—five possible answers)

3. *Think back to the last time you felt disappointed or frustrated with people in your congregation. What did you do—if anything—to address the challenges you faced?* (open-ended question)

Study Two

The Barna Group surveyed by phone 1,005 U.S. adults (over age eighteen) in October 2008 in their OmniPoll using CATI (see above). The cooperation rate was 63 percent, on par with the industry norm of 60 percent. The sampling error was +/– three points.

The adults surveyed came from within the forty-eight continental United States and represented a cross section of ages, genders, education, household income, marital status, and denominations. Six hundred and fifty identified themselves as Christian. This survey, which provided a fascinating look at how well the people in the pew understand our frustrations, asked one question:

> *Some pastors experience frustration or disappointment with the people who attend the church they pastor. Thinking about the church you attend most often, what is it about the people or that congregation that is most likely to cause frustration or disappointment for the senior pastor of the church?*

Study Three

LifeWay Research (the research arm of the Southern Baptist Convention) surveyed a representative sample of over 1,000 Protestant pastors in October 2008. The sampling error was +/– 3.1 percent. The cooperation rate was 89 percent for question one and 85 percent for question two.

The pastors surveyed represent a cross section of ages, denominations, church sizes, and church ages.

It was interesting to see how closely the results from question one of the Barna Group's first survey mirrored the results of question one from this survey. In effect, when both are combined, the sampling pool more than doubles. This survey asked these two questions:

1. *Think about the challenges pastors often face when it comes to their relationships with people who attend their church. For you, what are the types of issues that cause the most disappointments or frustrations between you and the people in your church?* (open-ended question)
2. *Please briefly describe what the people in your church could do differently to make your ministry in your church more joyful for you.* (open-ended question)

Study Four

This study, conducted through Christianity Today's National ChristianPoll.com in January 2009, falls into a different category than the other three. It reflects 284 completed online surveys of pastors that periodically take surveys. The response rate among pastors on this panel was 49 percent, with an error rate of +/– 5.8 percent.

Although not as scientific and random as the other surveys, it provided some fascinating insights. The pastors who responded came from churches of various sizes (average attendance 236) and tenure, and their average age was fifty-one. This survey asked these five questions:

1. *Think about the challenges you as a pastor often face when it comes to your relationships with the people in your church. When you consider the types of issues that cause the most disappointments or frustrations, would you have entered the ministry if you had known*

ahead of time you'd face these issues? (closed-ended question—three possible answers)

2. *To what extent do you believe the people in your church know and understand the frustrations and disappointments their behavior or attitude brings to you as their pastor?* (closed-ended question—four possible answers)
3. *What group of people in your church causes you the greatest frustration and disappointment?* (closed-ended question—eight possible answers)
4. *Think about what people in your church have done for you that has personally encouraged and affirmed you as a pastor. Briefly describe the experience you would say affirmed you the most.* (open-ended question)
5. *Share a story about a personal experience in your church (current or past) that has caused frustration and disappointment.* (open-ended question)

NOTES

Introduction

1. Details from *Leadership Journal*, "Preacher in the Hands of an Angry Church" (1/1/03). *www.ctlibrary.com/le/2003/winter/8.52.html*

Chapter 1

1. Pete Scazzero, "Beating the Pastoral Blues" (1/1/98). *www.christianity today.com/le/1998/winter/8l1063.html,* 1.
2. See Isaiah 6.
3. George Barna, *Revolution* (Carol Stream, IL: Tyndale, 2006), 14.
4. *Bit of Smoke,* "Quitting Church" (April 20, 2005). *http://bitofsmoke .wordpress.com/2005/04/*
5. Ellison Research, "One-Third of All Churchgoers Have Less Than Full Loyalty to Their Church" (2/8/07). *www.ellisonresearch.com/ releases/20070208.htm*
6. Libby Lovelace, LifeWay, "The New View of Young Adults." *www .lifeway.com/article/?id=164481*
7. LifeWay, "LifeWay Research Surveys Formerly Churched; Can the Church Close the Back Door?" (Part 1 of 2). *www.lifeway.com/ article/?id=163612*
8. Pew Research Publications, "The U.S. Religious Landscape Survey

Reveals a Fluid and Diverse Pattern of Faith" (2/25/08). *http://pewresearch.org/pubs/743/united-states-religion*

Chapter 2

1. John Grisham, *The Partner* (New York: Random, 2005), 243.
2. Details from *http://science.ksc.nasa.gov/history/apollo/apollo-13/apollo-13.html*
3. David Kinnaman, *unChristian* (Grand Rapids: Baker, 2007), 42.
4. Gary Kinnaman and Alfred Ells, *Leaders that Last* (Grand Rapids: Baker, 2003), 96.
5. Blaine Allen, *Before You Quit* (Grand Rapids: Kregel, 2001), 5.
6. Four percent of pastors indicated they did not know of any issues, or had none.
7. Christianity Today International Church Research Report, *The Work Week of a Pastor*, 1997, 23.
8. Ellison Research, "Study Shows How Pastors Grade Their Own Church's Performance" (8/23/02). *www.ellisonresearch.com/ERPS%20II/Release%203%20Grades.htm*
9. Dr. James Dobson, Focus on the Family, "The Titanic. The Church. What They Have in Common" (August 1998). *www2.focusonthefamily.com/docstudy/newsletters/A000000803.cfm*
10. Hartford Institute for Religion Research, "Fast Facts." *http://hirr.hartsem.edu/research/fastfacts/fast_facts.html#denom*
11. Julia Duin, *Quitting Church* (Grand Rapids: Baker, 2008), 11.
12. Scott Thumma and Dave Travis, *Beyond Megachurch Myths: What We Can Learn From America's Largest Churches* (San Francisco: Jossey-Bass, 2007), 4.
13. Duin, 24.
14. Cathy Lynn Grossman, *USA Today*, "Survey: Americans Freely Change, or Drop, Their Religions" (5/30/08). *www.usatoday.com/news/religion/2008-02-25-survey_N.htm*
15. James P. Wind, The Alban Institute, "Crunching the

Numbers" (3/10/08). *www.alban.org/conversation.aspx?q=printme&id=5818*

16. Cathy Lynn Grossman, *USA Today*, "Most Religious Groups in USA Have Lost Ground, Survey Finds" (3/17/09). *www.usatoday.com/news/religion/2009-03-09-american-religion-ARIS_N.htm*
17. In Duin, 31.
18. Patton Dodd, "Why Men Don't Like Church." *www.beliefnet.com/Faiths/Christianity/2007/09/Why-Men-Dont-Like-Church.aspx*
19. Michael Lindsay, *Friendship: Creating a Culture of Connectivity in Your Church* (Loveland, CO: Group Publishing, Inc., 2005), 83.
20. LifeWay, "Study of Adults Who Switch Churches: Why They Flee." *www.lifeway.com/article/?id=165175*
21. Thumma and Travis, 1.
22. Hillary Wicai, *Baptist Standard,* "Ill-Behaving Members Lead to Clergy Burnout" (4/23/01). *www.baptiststandard.com/2001/4_23/pages/burnout.html*

Chapter 3

1. Francis Chan, *Crazy Love* (Colorado Springs: David C. Cook, 2008), 66.
2. Christianity Today International Church Research Report, *The Work Week of a Pastor*, 1997, 5.
3. Wayne Cordeiro, *Leading on Empty* (Minneapolis: Bethany House, 2009).
4. Anne Jackson and Craig Groeschel, *Mad Church Disease: Overcoming the Burnout Epidemic* (Grand Rapids: Zondervan, 2009).
5. From a personal interview.
6. Isaiah 61:3 NLT
7. Daniel Goleman, Richard E. Boyatzis, and Annie McKee, *Primal Leadership: Learning to Lead with Emotional Intelligence* (Waterton, MA: Harvard Business School Press, 2004), 112.
8. D. Scott Barfoot, Dr. Bruce Winston, and Dr. Charles Wickman,

Forced Pastoral Exits: An Exploratory Study (*www.pastorinresidence.org/newsletter/SurveyPIR.pdf*).

9. Eric Reed, *LeadershipJournal.net*, "Restoring Fallen Pastors" (1/1/06). *www.christianitytoday.com/le/2006/winter/22.21.html?start=1*
10. Dean R. Hoge and Jacqueline E. Wenger, *Pulpit & Pew*, "Experiences of Protestant Ministers Who Left Local Church Ministry" (10/25/03). *www.pulpitandpew.duke.edu/Hoge.pdf*
11. Christianity Today, *The Work Week of a Pastor*, 18.
12. *Grow Magazine*, "Rate of Attrition of New Nazarene Pastors" (Fall 2002). *www.growmagazine.org/archive/fall2002/default.html#rate*
13. Dobson, Focus on the Family, "The Titanic. The Church. What They Have in Common."
14. Focus on the Family, "Pastoral Ministries 2009 Survey." *www.parsonage.org/images/pdf/2009PMSurvey.pdf*, 5.
15. From personal correspondence.
16. Dr. Becky McMillan, *Pulpit & Pew*, "The View from Pulpit & Pew: Provocative Findings on Pastoral Leadership in the 21st Century" (2/21/03): 7.
17. 1 Kings 19:3–4 The Message
18. *www.pastorserve.net*
19. Tom W. Smith, NORC/University of Chicago, "Job Satisfaction in the United States" (4/17/07). *www-news.uchicago.edu/releases/07/pdf/070417.jobs.pdf*
20. L. Gregory Jones, *Pulpit & Pew*, "A Satisfying Vocation?" (August 2002). *www.pulpitandpew.duke.edu/xcentury.htm*
21. Ibid.
22. David Roach and Staff, LifeWay Research, "Bad Economy Challenges Churches but Provides Opportunities" (2009). *www.lifeway.com/article/?id-168985.*
23. Thumma and Travis, 184.
24. Christian Smith, Michael O. Emerson, and Patricia Snell, *Passing the Plate: Why American Christians Don't Give Away More Money* (New

York: Oxford University Press, 2008).

25. Jennifer Reingold, *CNNMoney.com,* "Jim Collins: How Great Companies Turn Crisis Into Opportunity" (1/22/09). *http://money.cnn.com/2009/01/15/news/companies/Jim_Collins_Crisis.fortune/index.htm*
26. *REV.org,* "Clergy Careers at Risk" (August 2005). *http://rev.org/protected/Article.aspx?ID=361*
27. Patricia Chang, Hartford Institute for Religion Research, "The Clergy Job Market: What Are the Opportunities for Ministry in the 21st Century?" (May 2003). *http://hirr.hartsem.edu/leadership/clergyresources_clergyjobs.html*
28. Patricia Chang, *Pulpit & Pew,* "Factors Shaping Clergy Careers" (2005). *www.pulpitandpew.duke.edu/clergycareers.html*
29. Alan Nelson, *REV.org,* "What's Eating Our Lunch?" (Jan/Feb 2009). *www.rev.org/article.asp?ID=3090*
30. Emphasis mine.

Chapter 4

1. Again, I didn't intend this book solely to document our problems; I wrote it primarily to focus on solutions.
2. LifeWay used sixty-eight subcategories; Barna Group combined theirs into sixteen, with verbal descriptions for each that further defined the subcategory.
3. Totals exceeded 100 percent because multiple responses were permitted.
4. November 2007, 68 subcategories; N=615 (number surveyed)
5. November 2008, 16 subcategories; N=1,002 (number surveyed)
6. Warren Bird, Leadership Network, "Teacher First: Leadership Network's 2009 Large-Church Senior Pastor Survey" (July 2009). *www.churchcentral.com/whitepapers/Teacher-First:-Leadership-Network's-2009-Survey-of-Large-Church-Senior-Pastors.*
7. Alan Nelson, *REV Magazine,* "Me to We" (Sept/Oct 2007): 68.
8. Luke 10:27

9. Bill Hull, "Leadership: It's Just Not Working" (7/1/05). *www.christianitytoday.com/global/printer.html?/le/2005/summer/6.26.html*
10. John 6:66
11. See Exodus 18.
12. Acts 6:2–4 NLT
13. Matthew 16:23
14. January 2009. The total exceeds 100 percent because multiple responses were permitted.

Chapter 5

1. In David Wood, "Committing to Mutuality, Congregations" (May/June 2002): no. 3. *www.alban.org/conversation.aspx?q=printme&id=3280*, 4.
2. See 1 Samuel 21.
3. Among the 615 surveyed, multiple responses were permitted, bringing the total to more than 100 percent.
4. KJV
5. See 1 Peter 4:8 NKJV.

Chapter 6

1. Henri J. M. Nouwen, *In the Name of Jesus* (New York: Crossroad, 1989), 32.
2. Verses 33–34
3. 1 Peter 5:3 NLT
4. Psalm 105:15
5. 1 Thessalonians 5:12
6. The Messsage
7. You'll see that this chart slightly differs from the earlier Mega-Themes chart. I've separated the "leadership/directional issues" component (number 3) from "church commitment issues," and I've included the "no frustrations/I don't know" category. (In the earlier description, I combined leadership/commitment issues and excluded "no frustrations/I don't know.")

8. Totals equal more than 100 percent because multiple answers were allowed.
9. Barna Group, 615 surveyed.
10. LifeWay, 1,002 surveyed.
11. Barna Group, 650 surveyed.
12. H. B. London, *Pastors at Greater Risk* (Ventura, CA: Regal, 2003).
13. From personal correspondence, 1/20/09.
14. I excluded the "I don't know/I have no problems" category, although 18 percent gave that answer.
15. LifeWay, 2008; 1,002 surveyed.
16. Totals equal more than 100 percent because multiple answers were allowed.
17. Barna Group, 615 surveyed; LifeWay, 1,002 surveyed.
18. Barna Group, 650 surveyed.
19. Lifeway, 1,002 surveyed.
20. NationalChristianPoll.com, 2009, 255 surveyed.
21. Focus on the Family, "Pastoral Ministries 2009 Survey" (of more than two thousand pastors), *www.parsonage.org/images/pdf/2009PMSurvey.pdf*, 11.
22. From a personal interview.

Chapter 7

1. Craig Groeschel, *Confessions of a Pastor* (Colorado Springs: Multnomah, 2006), 60.
2. See 1 Kings 19.
3. Mark McMinn, et al., *Pastoral Psychology*, "Care for Pastors: Learning from Clergy and Their Spouses," 53:6 (July 2005): 563–79.
4. Ibid., 578.
5. Proverbs 27:17
6. Ecclesiastes 4:7, 9–12 NLT
7. Proverbs 11:14 The Message

8. Philippians 2:25; 2:19ff; Colossians 4:7, 10ff; 2 Timothy 4:11
9. Kinnaman and Ells, *Leaders that Last*, 10.
10. REV.org, "Steve Arterburn Interview: Open Season" (August 2007). *http://rev.org/protected/Article.aspx?ID=2519*
11. Focus on the Family, "Pastoral Ministries 2009 Survey," 8.
12. Michael Jinkins, The Alban Institute, *Congregations,* "Great Expectation, Sobering Realities: Findings From a New Study on Clergy Burnout, (May/June 2002): No. 3. *www.alban.org/conversation.aspx?q=printme&id=3284*
13. The Barna Group, "Pastors Feel Confident in Ministry, But Many Struggle in Their Interaction with Others" (7/10/06). *www.barna.org/barna-update/article/17-leadership/150-pastors-feel-confident-in-ministry-but-many-struggle-in-their-interaction-with-others*
14. Henry Cloud and John Townsend, *Safe People* (Grand Rapids: Zondervan, 1995), 129.
15. Adapted from ibid.
16. Daniel Goleman, *Emotional Intelligence* (New York: Bantam, 2006).
17. Goleman, Boyatzis, and McKee, *Primal Leadership*, 6–7.
18. Ibid., 112.
19. 1 Samuel 16:7 The Message
20. Psalm 101:6 The Message
21. Psalm 141:5 NLT
22. Goleman, Boyatzis, and McKee, *Primal Leadership,* 94.
23. 1 Corinthians 8:1 CEV
24. James 4:2
25. James 1:5 NLT
26. J. Robert Clinton and Paul D. Stanley, *Connecting: The Mentoring Relationships You Need to Succeed in Life* (Colorado Springs: NavPress, 1992), 159.
27. Bill Hybels, *Courageous Leadership* (Grand Rapids: Baker, 2003), 249.

Chapter 8

1. Tim Keller, The Gospel Coalition, "Talking About Idolatry in a Postmodern Age" (April 2007). *www.monergism.com/postmodernidols .html*
2. Jack Hayford, *LeadershipJournal.net,* "How Many Did You Have Last Sunday?" (1/1/98). *www.christianitytoday.com/le/1998/winter/8l1039 .html*
3. Bill Hull, *LeadershipJournal.net,* "It's Just Not Working" (7/1/05). *www.christianitytoday.com/le/2005/summer/6.26.html*
4. The Barna Group, "Survey Shows Pastors Claim Congregants Are Deeply Committed to God," *The Barna Update* (1/10/06). *www .barna.org/barna-update/article/5-barna-update/165-surveys-show-pastors-claim-congregants-are-deeply-committed-to-god-but-congregants-deny-it*
5. Ibid.
6. NLT
7. From a personal interview.
8. Rev. Dr. James P. Wind, "The Leading Edge: A Fresh Look at American Clergy," *Congregations* (May/June 2002). *www.alban.org/conversation.aspx?q=printme&id=3290*, 2.
9. Ellison Research, "New research shows pastors may not have a realistic view of the health of their own family," 870 surveyed (7/19/05). *www.ellisonresearch.com/ERPS%20II/release_17_family.htm*
10. Goleman, Boyatzis, and McKee, *Primal Leadership*, 92.
11. Luke 10:38–42
12. Jeremiah 9:1
13. Jeremiah 1:19
14. Philippians 1:25
15. 2 Corinthians 12:9
16. Luke 13:34
17. David L. Goetz, *Death by Suburb* (New York: HarperCollins, 2006), 121.
18. 1 Thessalonians 2:10–12

19. 2 Corinthians 5:2 THE MESSAGE
20. ESV
21. D. A. Carson, *The Cross and Christian Ministry* (Grand Rapids: Baker, 2004), 80.

CHAPTER 9

1. Nouwen, *In the Name of Jesus,* 20.
2. Nouwen, 77.
3. Henry Cloud, *Integrity* (New York: HarperCollins, 2006), 31.
4. The sum of the totals exceeds 100 percent because of overlapping answers.
5. Gary McIntosh and Samuel Rima, *Overcoming the Dark Side of Leadership* (Grand Rapids: Baker, 1997), 29.
6. Ibid., 48.
7. 1 Corinthians 4:1–4 NLT
8. Scazzero, "Beating the Pastoral Blues," 2.
9. Julia Duin, *Quitting Church,* 11.
10. In David Wood, "Committing to Mutuality," *Congregations* (May/June 2002): no. 3, *www.alban.org/conversation.aspx?q=printme&id=3280,* 3.
11. 2 Corinthians 12:9–10
12. Scazzero, "Beating the Pastoral Blues," 3.
13. Henry Cloud and John Townsend, *Boundaries: When to Say Yes, When to Say No, to Take Control of Your Life* (Grand Rapids: Zondervan, 2001).
14. Goleman, Boyatzis, and McKee, *Primal Leadership*, 34.
15. In Wood, "Committing to Mutuality: An Interview with Eugene Peterson."
16. Clive Thompson, *The New York Times*, "Meet the Life Hackers" (10/16/05). *www.nytimes.com/2005/10/16/magazine/16guru.html*
17. Nouwen, *In the Name of Jesus,* 28.
18. Ibid., 53.

Chapter 10

1. In Wayne Cordeiro, *Leading on Empty*, 81.
2. Adapted
3. Mark 8:34
4. Luke 14:26
5. 1 Peter 5:2 NLT
6. Matthew 10:39 The Message
7. Galatians 6:2
8. Galatians 6:5
9. Mark 6:31
10. Mark 12:31
11. Cloud and Townsend, *Boundaries*, 107.
12. Anne Jackson, *Mad Church Disease* (Grand Rapids: Zondervan, 2009), 117.
13. Previously, I grouped the LifeWay research into three categories of things pastors said they wanted their churches to do differently. I clustered those responses into similar groupings that the other research discovered were the three major frustration areas (church/leadership issues, spiritual-growth issues, and relationship issues). But to help particularize what they'd want different *in their setting*, I've expanded responses into several groupings, combining the LifeWay responses with the NationalChristianpoll.com responses.
14. In David Wood, 2.
15. Ibid., 3.
16. Craig Groeschel, "Full-Time Pastor but Only Part-Time Follower of Jesus" (4/1/07). *www.christianitytoday.com/le/2007/spring/1.25.html*
17. 2 Timothy 4:2 NLT
18. In the next chapter, we dialogue about the unique frustrations and ministry killers pastors' wives face.
19. 1 Corinthians 16:18

20. 2 Corinthians 7:13
21. 2 Timothy 1:16
22. Philemon 7
23. Matthew 11:28
24. Luke 6:38 The Message

Chapter 11

1. From *www.pastorswife.net/*
2. Psalm 118:24
3. *Time* magazine, "Pastors' Wives Come Together" (3/29/07). *www.time.com/time/magazine/article/0,9171,1604902,00.html?artId=1604902?contType=article?chn=us*
4. Ibid.
5. Dr. Jama Davis, Liberty University Digital Commons, *Alone in a Crowd: A Phenomenological Inquiry into Loneliness as Experienced by Pastors' Wives,* Liberty University, May 2007. *http://digitalcommons.liberty.edu/doctoral/49/*
6. Genesis 50:20 NLT
7. Mark McMinn, et al., *Pastoral Psychology,* "Care for Pastors: Learning from Clergy and Their Spouses" (53:6, July 2005): 563–79.

Chapter 12

1. Richard J. Foster, *Prayer* (New York: HarperCollins, 2002), 21.
2. In Foster, 62.
3. *www.goodreads.com/author/quotes/229.Abraham_Lincoln?page=5*
4. Matthew 11:28
5. Thomas Kelly, *A Testament of Devotion* (New York: Harper & Row, 1941), 124.
6. John 12:24 NASB
7. Søren Kierkegaard, *The Journals of Kierkegaard,* ed. Alexander Dru (New York: Harper & Brothers, 1959), 245.
8. Richard Foster, 55.

9. A. W. Tozer, *The Pursuit of God,* compiler Edythe Draper (Camp Hill, PA: Christian Publications, Inc., 1995), 98.
10. Psalm 27:8 The Message
11. Tozer, 183.
12. Matthew 25:14–30
13. 1 Corinthians 12
14. David Goetz, 43.
15. In Victor Parachin, *Today's Christian,* "8 Ways to Encourage Your Pastor" (Sept/Oct. 1999). *www.christianitytoday.com/tc/1999/sepoct/9r5035.html?start=1*
16. Sam Storms, *The Hope of Glory* (Wheaton, IL: Crossway, 2001), 135.
17. 2 Corinthians 4:16, 18
18. Colossians 1:29
19. NLT
20. Goetz, 198

ACKNOWLEDGMENTS

Thanks to my wife, Sherryl, for her patience during the many hours when my writing kept me preoccupied.

Thanks to Kyle Duncan, executive editor at Bethany House, for giving me the privilege of writing for a great company.

Thanks to Steve Laube, my agent, for believing in a fledgling writer several years ago.

Thanks to Christopher Soderstrom, my editor, who helped make me a better writer.

Thanks to Rebeca Seitz, my publicist, for her diligence in getting the word out.

Thanks to Daryl McMullen, my Web designer, for creating a compelling Web site.

Thanks to Kyle Zehr and Zach Montroy, two fellow staffers, for a super job in creating the book's video.